SUMMIT PIONEERS

Alison Grabau

Photography by
Bob Winsett

Cover Photo Courtesy of Frances Long.

SUMMIT PIONEERS

Proceeds to Benefit

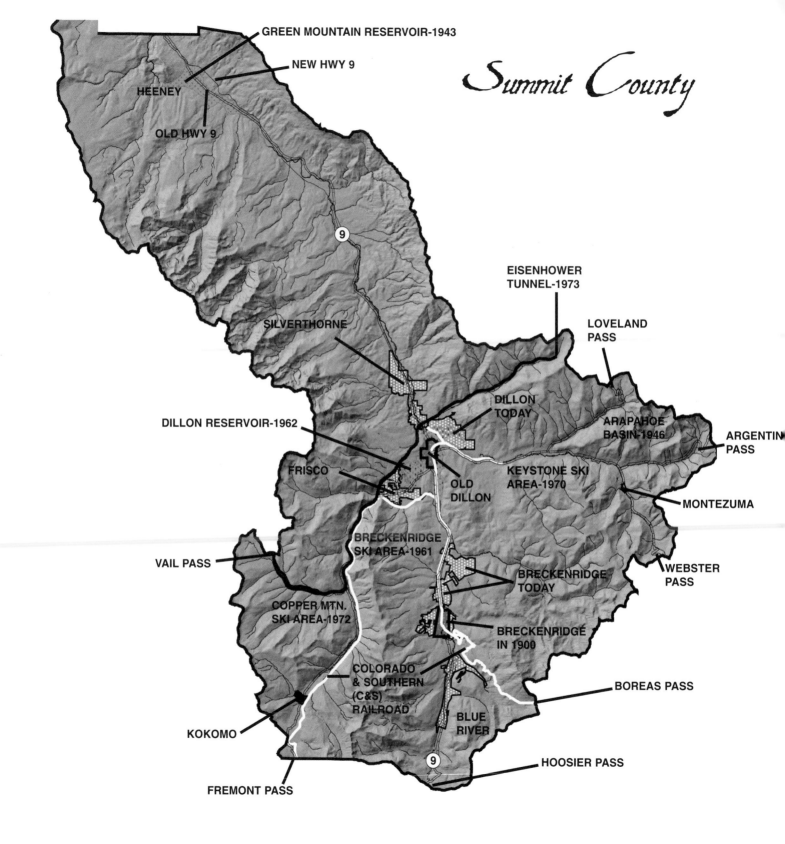

Summit County

GREEN MOUNTAIN RESERVOIR-1943

NEW HWY 9

HEENEY

OLD HWY 9

EISENHOWER TUNNEL-1973

LOVELAND PASS

SILVERTHORNE

DILLON TODAY

ARAPAHOE BASIN-1946

ARGENTIN PASS

DILLON RESERVOIR-1962

FRISCO

OLD DILLON

KEYSTONE SKI AREA-1970

MONTEZUMA

VAIL PASS

BRECKENRIDGE SKI AREA-1961

BRECKENRIDGE TODAY

WEBSTER PASS

COPPER MTN. SKI AREA-1972

BRECKENRIDGE IN 1900

COLORADO & SOUTHERN (C&S) RAILROAD

BOREAS PASS

KOKOMO

BLUE RIVER

FREMONT PASS

HOOSIER PASS

Table of Contents

Forward	ii
Summit Foundation	iv
Acknowledgements	v
Bios	vi
Introduction	viii
Karl and Jean Knorr	1
Helen Foote	7
Freda Langell Nieters	13
Howard Giberson	19
Jim Bowden	23
Bernie and Linda McMenamy	29
Joe Bailey	35
Sue (Giberson) Chamberlain	41
Max and Edna Dercum	47
Bill Bergman	53
Jody Anderson and Phyllis Armstrong	59
Bob Craig	65
Gene and Ina Gillis	71
Gert (Culbreath) Young	77
Bud and Martha Enyeart	85
Chris Beger	91
Grady and Gail Culbreath	95
Olav Pedersen	101
Marie Zdechlik	107
Alf Tieze	113
Melvin and Frances Long	119
Trygve Berge	125
George and Susy Culbreath	131
Gertrude Philippe	137
Jim and Maureen Nicholls	143
Sena Valaer	151
Afterward	159

Forward

It first occurred to me about four or five years ago that it might be interesting to chronicle Summit County's past as seen through the eyes of its remaining contemporary pioneers. The idea of interviewing and photographing some of the old-timers from around Summit County had a certain amount of appeal and seemed like a worthwhile undertaking. Unfortunately, it was years later before I acted on the idea.

In the spring of 1998 while working on a project for Keystone Resort, the idea resurfaced, this time with more urgency. It suddenly seemed imperative that the process of photographing and interviewing begin before the opportunity to do so with any of the potential subjects of this book be lost for good, their stories having gone untold.

I initiated a meeting with long-time residents Hank Parker, Meg Lass and Tony Wilson as well as newcomer Alison Grabau. Meg and Tony are owners of Wilson•Lass Creative Communications, Inc. in Breckenridge and very "community sensitive" people with whom I have worked for the last 10 years. Alison began working with Wilson•Lass Creative Communications in 1997.

A list of subjects to interview was drawn up and a loose framework for the book discussed. We put together a strategy for introducing ourselves and the idea behind the book to those people on our list. Still, it was hard to make the initial cold-call to the first person on the list. After talking at length with another long-time local, Mark Jones, he suggested that he could break the ice with a few of the people to be interviewed. I was (and still am) grateful for his efforts. The process had begun.

Cold-calling people and explaining the idea behind this book project did not come easily. I am thankful that each person we called was receptive enough to allow Alison and me into their homes for the initial interview. As Mark had foreseen, once we interviewed a few of the people on the list, word would spread among many of the others that the project was afoot and, hopefully, that it was one worth participating in.

We were, at first, quite surprised that many of the people contacted could not understand why their lives might be interesting to others. Once the interview process had begun, however, most seemed to find it, at the very least, mildly cathartic to recount days gone by. Some found a great deal of pleasure in the process while others responded more modestly to the gently probing questions thought up and asked by Alison. Without a doubt, each story in the book is unique in its point of view even though the lives of many of the people did – and still do – overlap.

Alison and I are profoundly grateful to each and every person in this book for their patience and time. That there was life in Summit County before tourism and the ski resort business arrived seems increasingly important to relate given the priority that development is now given in Summit County. The contributions to the ski resort business that many of the people in this book made while that business was in its infancy are remarkable. While the future of Summit County is not entirely clear, it seems at times to be more readily visible than its past. Thanks to the recollections of those who came before, perhaps we can get at least a glimpse into the lives and times of those who built the foundation on which Summit County rests today.

In the book *Platte River*, one of author Rick Bass's characters related, "Even now, so many days and years later, I remember things that I had forgotten, that I thought were gone forever. The job is never done for it is only us, here on this piece of land; everything else is being washed away or changing. We are bedrock, however; she wants us to be bedrock, and that requires memory, and storytelling, to those who will someday be the new bedrock. . . ."

Bob Winsett
August, 1999

The Summit Foundation

Celebrating 15 years of giving in 1999, The Summit Foundation is a community foundation dedicated to improving the quality of life for residents and guests of Summit County. Since 1986, the Foundation has awarded more than $2.6 million in grants and scholarships. The cornerstone for The Summit Foundation's fundraising is the Patron Pass program, anchored by transferable season ski passes generously donated by Arapahoe Basin Ski Area, Breckenridge Ski Resort, Copper Mountain Resort and Keystone Resort, as well as Vail Mountain and Beaver Creek. Additional funding comes from a variety of special events and projects. *Summit Pioneers* pays tribute to the early pioneers of Summit County and celebrates their gifts to the community. Like these individuals who have contributed so much to this County's rich heritage, all proceeds from *Summit Pioneers* are being dedicated to The Summit Foundation's Endowment Fund.

Acknowledgements

Thanks to the following people for their suggestions, input and vision: Hank Parker, Tony Wilson, Meg Lass, Rebecca Waugh, Mark Jones, Nancy Follett, Phil and Janelle Kopp, Mary Staby and Chuck Julin. Thanks also to friend and neighbor Ron Sheller for the map. We would like to express our gratitude to the family of Bruce Schaeffer for his photos of Jim Bowden. We are deeply indebted to Kim DiLallo and Deb Edwards of The Summit Foundation for their support and encouragement. Without the hard work of Lori O'Bryan, Keith Dudley, Carrie Welch and Denise Dionne of Wilson · Lass Creative Communications, this book would never have been published. Thanks to Beth Sharp, Rachel Flood and Susan Kelley for many hours spent reading every story in this book. We would also like to express our appreciation to Columbine Gallery and Anthony's of Frisco for their assistance and financial help along the way. Finally, a heartfelt thanks to Brent Doerzman and Ed Cies of Cies Sexton Photographics for their technical and financial support.

Bios

Wilson · Lass Creative Communications, Inc.

Founded by Tony Wilson and Meg Lass in Breckenridge in 1981, Wilson · Lass began as a design firm that would put the fun and beauty back into visual communications. Today, Wilson · Lass has become a leading communications company by establishing trusted, personal relationships with their clients and working with them to increase their revenues and marketshare. Its staff of seven core team members, Meg, Tony, Alison Grabau, Lori O'Bryan, Denise Dionne, Keith Dudley and Kate Johnson, as well as its cadre of freelance talent, have the capabilities for generating a wide range of tailored, creative offerings. Wilson · Lass enjoys a convenient location in the heart of Breckenridge and a passion for high-altitude living that offers them the keen insight to the mountain culture and lifestyle, especially in the sports and recreation, hospitality, real estate development and resort industries. It is the appreciation for Summit County's rich heritage that inspires Wilson · Lass to give back to the community that has given so much to them.

Alison Grabau

Originally from Boone, Iowa, Alison earned her journalism and history (honors) degrees at the University of Kansas and is currently working on her Masters of Business Administration through the University of Denver. She has worked on the editorial staffs of *Women's Sports & Fitness* magazine, *Midwestern Living* magazine, *ICON* magazine, Metropolitan State College of Denver publications and as a beat reporter for a small newspaper. Over the years she has also done a great deal of freelance writing. Currently, she is the client services director for Wilson · Lass Creative Communications, Inc. in Breckenridge. Whenever possible, Alison enjoys hiking or snow-shoeing near her home in Blue River with her yellow lab, Bella.

Bob Winsett

Colorado native Bob Winsett has been a freelance commercial photographer in Summit County since leaving the ski business behind 12 years ago. His photos have appeared in many regional and national magazines including *U.S. News and World Report*, *Snow Country*, *Outdoor Life*, *Powder* and *Forbes*. He is represented by Index Stock Imagery in New York City. His photos from the Himalayan country of Bhutan were recently featured at the Telluride Mountain Film Festival this past spring. Bob's relationship with Wilson · Lass as well as his affinity for photographing people in their environments have been the driving forces behind the creation of this book.

Introduction

Photographer Bob Winsett asked himself one day, "Wouldn't it be interesting to photograph and interview a few of the old-timers in Frisco?" A few years later, while working on a project for Keystone Resort, a similar idea came to him, but this time, with a sense of urgency. He suddenly realized that, with the rapid urbanization of Summit County, it was more important than ever to record the evolution of the County's contemporary history before the untold stories were lost forever.

Working with the talented staff of Wilson·Lass Creative Communications of Breckenridge, Bob's brainchild has since evolved into *Summit Pioneers* – "compendium of memoirs" that is accompanied by photographs from 26 engaging characters whose lives have helped to shape Summit County, Colorado.

Working as volunteers, the book's contributors initially took on the project for themselves. Their subjects were their neighbors and members of the community where they live. For this group, there was no arranging or inventing; everything was spontaneous and took its own place. It was like riding through familiar terrain on a horse that knew the way. Consequently, *Summit Pioneers* is both notable and enduring. It is a great gift and a fine thing.

The photography in the book is a mix of contemporary portraits by Bob Winsett and historical photographs from the featured families. Many of the historical photographs depict people and other living things in the natural environment, with light, and the freedom of wide-open spaces around them. The subjects melt into the landscape until they are not photographic images at all, but life itself. Bob's intimate portraits also have great dramatic power. His subjects are tightly framed, sharply focused and full of life. This intensity comes through Bob's great gift of observation and his simplicity in style and honesty of treatment.

The mood and theme of the publication are distinguished by the land, the epic labors of the modern-day pioneers and the romantic exaltations of their early accomplishments. Tony Wilson, the book's creative director, credits the "pioneers" and their "impelling" stories as a direct source of inspiration. The coming together of the text, photography and subjects "as a whole piece" was a source of graphic enlightenment for: Tony, Art Director Denise Dionne, former Production Artist Keith Dudley and Assistant Art Director Carrie Welch. For Tony, this was an important creative experience because the content seemed to dictate the form the book would take – a work that was not plotted by design itself.

Journalist Alison Grabau, who spent 14 months with Bob Winsett interviewing subjects, also thought about the book's structure and style a great deal. However, she too found that the structure was something dictated by the subjects, and the narrative, literally, shaped itself.

Alison was especially thrilled by the accounts of a birth of a new land and awed with how "rugged" earlier life was in Summit County, Colorado. She found in her subjects the memories of the struggles to tame the wild land, the storms of winter, the tending of livestock, the exhilarating labors of a new ski industry. These 26 selected individuals are only a few of the community leaders who embodied the creative instincts, the will and the foresight necessary to bring the unbroken country into cultural refinement. Their true stories are more dramatic and interesting than anything we could have invented. Many of the tales were remembered, but not documented until now.

Summit Pioneers is autobiographical because the subjects are actual people we know. It is close to life. For many, the book is about old neighbors and acquaintances. Newcomers, however, will read about a Summit County that they will never know.

The influence of Summit County's geography is especially strong in the work. The land is the hero. Perhaps that is why many of the contemporary pioneers point to certain natural features of the area as identifiable keystones in their lives. The book's photographs and text reflect nature's artistic treatment of the diverse landscape – the land of hay fields and wildflower meadows, great expanses of sky, climatic extremes, towering pine forests and snow-covered mountain slopes. In *Summit Pioneers*, we also see people at their labors and at play together, experiencing joys and sorrows that are communal. In this stylized presentation of a land and its people, experience, photography, graphic design and writing fuse together as dynamic elements of art.

Summit Pioneers celebrates the continuous growth as experienced by Summit County's 20th-century ranchers, town builders, and resort, environmental and ski pioneers. The book profiles individuals who adapted themselves to new conditions, identifying themselves with the Rocky Mountain terrain and becoming voices in their community. It introduces a new kind of story and brings a new perspective to Summit County's history. The book discloses the splendid human resources of the area's population and the changing face of the County.

Summit Pioneers is a nostalgic account of a respectful way of life lived close to the land. The work not only signals continuity between old and new generations, but applies an aesthetic approach to other subjects, such as rural labors, youthful romance, the role of the land and the love of one's country. Even so, the book does not deal with grand ideas, nor does it dazzle by means of style. It possesses ordinary stories, yet the book has richness, charm and dignity. *Summit Pioneers* is true to life.

–Rebecca Waugh
County Preservation Coordinator, Historic Boulder, Inc. and the Town of Breckenridge
Formerly Museum Administrator of the Summit Historical Society

Karl and Jean Knorr

"When a young school marm showed up in the country,
she usually didn't get away."

—Karl Knorr on the ranchers who married school teachers

A ranch in the valley of the Lower Blue, halfway between Silverthorne and Kremmling, is perhaps the last place on earth anyone would expect to find a zebra, lion, gazelle or a 16-foot, striped blue marlin. Nevertheless, these exotic creatures are gathered in the den of Karl and Jean Knorr's ranch home as if to share the tales of adventurous travel in faraway lands. The Knorrs have collected a vast number of wild game trophies as testimony to their passion for hunting and fishing and their many trips to places like Alaska, Africa, Costa Rica, Canada and Mexico. Jean shot her first deer when she was 18 with her grandfather in Boulder, turning one of life's necessities into a sport that she and her husband still enjoy. Despite their apparent wanderlust and restless spirit, the Knorrs say that there is nothing better than coming home — home to the Colorado ranch that has always been the stable arm to their life's ever-swiveling protractor.

After growing up in Boulder and Longmont, Jean moved to the mountains and was teaching at Lakeside School when she met Karl. A photography buff, he had come to present a color slideshow to the children. "When a young school marm showed up in the country, she usually didn't get away," laughed Karl.

The community hall of the Lakeside precinct was often the setting for all sorts of community gatherings, such as elections, funerals and dances. It was at one of those dances when Karl first began playing the drums, as he would do for the next 12 to 15 years, that he and Jean began the courtship that resulted in their eventual marriage.

"I grew up in a community of hunters,
trappers and cowboys.
I liked it all."

Karl said, "We got together quite a bit in the winter with a piano and a fiddle and had ourselves a pretty good stomp."

Karl fondly remembers that he and other part-time musicians would end up traveling from Grand Lake to Fairplay and all the towns in between to play for the dances that were held almost every Saturday night. Jean explained that the women would make all the sandwiches, cakes and coffee for these social occasions while all the children would end up falling asleep on the benches in the cookhouse.

The Knorrs will attest that being "home on the range" involves an abundance of vigor, self-reliance and common sense. It requires a lot of hard work, sweat and determination with little financial return. Nevertheless, Karl said he liked every aspect of growing up on a ranch. "I grew up in a community of hunters, trappers and cowboys. I liked it all."

George (L) and Karl Knorr (R) circa 1916.

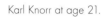

Karl Knorr at age 21.

L-R: George, Ted and Karl Knorr
circa 1915.

Karl's mother's father, Judge William Guyselman, arrived in Breckenridge around 1880 and soon after, acquired land down the Blue River. Karl's father came from Germany when he was 18, rather than complete his two years of required military service. He and his brother mined around Montezuma and Breckenridge. He built the building that today is the Knorr House outdoor recreation store in Breckenridge as a place for them to live. After awhile, they opened a saloon called the Knorr Brothers' Pioneer Saloon and operated it in the 1880s and 1890s until Karl's dad sold his portion to his brother in order to pursue ranching. He then married Judge Guyselman's daughter and moved to the current ranch in 1902.

"We got together quite a bit in the winter with a piano and a fiddle and had ourselves a pretty good stomp."

In the early part of the century, there were many ranches up and down the river until the Green Mountain Reservoir came along. The town of Heeney first emerged as a construction camp for all the reservoir workers, then turned into a town in the mid-1940s. Much of the Knorr's original ranch was displaced by the reservoir, which was built over three summers from 1940 to 1942. "We moved as many buildings as we could," Karl said, but the Green Mountain Reservoir provided no benefit that he could see to the cattle or ranching business.

"The ranch people kept on ranching, but it was quite a disruption," Karl explained. "We had to get out of there and start over. It was like a gopher scrambling to high ground when you try to drown him out."

Karl had two brothers, Ted, who was 10 years older, and George, just a year and a half older. Karl and George were inseparable. They went to grade school at Lakeside in the summertime for the first eight grades in the mid-1920s because traveling in the winter months was so difficult.

"Most of the country kids skied because that was a good way to get around," Karl said. "Either you got around on skis or webs (snowshoes), or on horses, but it was pretty tough to travel on foot in the snow."

After Karl and George graduated high school in 1930, they returned to the ranch. Karl said they both expected to return only to earn enough money for college, but their father died and the opportunity arose to purchase Mount Powell Ranch "dirt cheap." It was during The Great Depression and all of them knew the ranch was worth much more than they paid. "We were fortunate to start when we did," said Karl.

Karl Knorr and his early
Northland touring skis.

The ranch started small, but eventually, after adding to the land through various acquisitions, it became so large that it was too much work for Karl and his brother to handle alone. At one time, the Knorr brothers had approximately 10,000 acres and wintered as many as 700 to 800 cows. Karl explained that when he was a child, they would ship their cattle to Denver after a "good ole' cattle drive" to either Kremmling or Dillon where they would load them on a train. They also had 35 to 40 draft horses and a few saddle horses. His father used to raise and break teams of draft horses and sell them to the mines to pull ore wagons and sleds. Karl recalls one time when his brother injured his ankle while they were breaking foals and couldn't work for a few days. "I had more than 500 head of cattle to feed with just a pitchfork. Just a team of horses, a sled and a pitchfork!"

Karl explained how Lake Dillon had as much to do with tourism as anything else. About this time, alpine skiing began to emerge in the County as well, but the effects of the ski business were gradual. Karl grew up skiing. He was influenced by the old Norwegian jumpers such as Carl Howleson, the Haugen brothers and the Prestruds. He and his friends would jump at Slate Creek Ranch and Dillon. They also did plenty of cross-country skiing, as much for sport as for transportation.

"When we were kids, one guy would get up on the saddle horse and throw the end of the rope to the other guy who would be pulled from behind on skis," Karl remembers. He stopped skiing at age 82, but only because he injured himself when he didn't make a turn skijoring (being pulled on skis behind a horse) on sheer ice.

Today, Karl and Jean still own 2,200 acres and lease it out to people that they have known for years. Looking back, even in the shadow of their many travel souvenirs, it is life in Summit County that seems to hold the fondest memories for Karl.

"I had a happy childhood," he said. "Kids now a days, they get all sorts of toys. We had very few. But we didn't need many. We had a good time with the stuff we had. We had skis, horses, cattle, dogs and cats."

Helen Foote

*"I used to know the exact number of people and dogs in Frisco.
I think it was between 60 and 70."*

—*Helen Foote on Frisco in the 1940s*

Even with fewer than 70 people once living in Frisco, (Laura) Helen Foote was always in the heart of the town's social center. For 53 years, Helen has lived at 510 Main Street, which has served over the years as the town's general store, post office, gas station, communications center and meeting house.

Born on a farm in the Texas Panhandle, Helen married the neighbor boy, Robert S. Foote, in 1941. They moved to California for the majority of World War II while her husband worked for Vultee Aircraft. He was never drafted and by the War's end, she soon found herself on the road to Summit County, Colorado, caught up in her husband's vision of living in a cabin by the creek and fishing all the time. Fishing was a passion that she and Bob shared throughout their marriage and they began a bi-weekly ritual to fish in the north Ten Mile Canyon every Wednesday and Sunday afternoon. They also became among the first fishing guides in Summit County.

After a long trip to scout prospective property on two-lane gravel roads with their 3-year-old daughter, they were forced to spend the first night in Fairplay before arriving in Frisco.

"This part I remember distinctly," said Helen. "We spent the night in some cabin that had wood and coal heat and a great big cook stove. My husband would get up in the night and throw another log on the fire to try to keep us warm. There was a tea kettle with water in it that was sitting on the back of the stove, and yet, the room was so cold that the water in the kettle froze, despite the fire. I said, 'Boy, we sure don't want to live here!'"

"That first Halloween, I made a costume from gunny sacks and dressed my daughter up as a little monkey. It sure didn't take her long to go trick-or-treating because there weren't that many houses in town."

Frisco, originally named Frisco City, was founded during the height of the gold and silver mining boom. During mining's glory days, Frisco boasted 31 saloons, four hotels, two railroads, a 50-oven coke operation and numerous logging operations. It was a rollercoaster living through the many booms and busts that the community continually managed to survive. Mining's eventual collapse following World War I left the local residents scrambling to find alternative employment in areas such as logging or hunting.

Foote's Rest
on Main Street,
Frisco, in 1940.

Helen Foote (R) and her mother-in-law,
Hanna Nonnie Foote, in front of
Foote's Rest circa 1950.

In that first year or so, Helen sent her daughter Patty door to door delivering May baskets as a friendly gesture to their new neighbors. She also made every effort to get involved with the community while creating fun for her children in their remote mountain town. "That first Halloween, I made a costume from gunny sacks and dressed my daughter up as a little monkey," Helen recalled. "It sure didn't take her long to go trick-or-treating because there weren't all that many houses in town."

"Tourists rented the cabins for one night or one week at a time. If they were lucky enough to catch some fish during their stay, then they'd be sure to come back the next year. We met a lot of neat friends that way."

Unlike Dillon, which had neon lights lining its streets, Frisco was much darker because it didn't have the same lighting system. Frisco received electricity and street lights in 1901, but when the Excelsior mine ceased operation in the 1920s, these amenities were removed until many years later. Helen had the foresight to bring everything they owned when they moved from California, because there wouldn't be many stores to buy things once they arrived in the Rocky Mountains.

In 1946, Helen and Bob pooled resources with Bob's mother, Hanna Nonnie, to purchase eight lots for $6,500. In 1948, they finally received running water and a year later, indoor plumbing. On the property was a building, now Helen's home, that was built by a late 19th-century engineer and mining clerk, Louis A. Wildhack. In 1882, Wildhack built the one-story, 14-foot by 14-foot frame structure, with a wooden porch and false front, along Main Street to serve as his office and residence. In 1914, after a fire consumed the post office, Wildhack became Frisco's postmaster, using the Main Street house as its new location. A decade later, he added a two- and one-half-story addition onto the east side of the original structure to accommodate the store and post office using materials from the nearby Admiral Mine. It became the only general store in town and functioned as the social center of Frisco. Having one of the only two telephones in town in the early part of the century, Wildhack's store became the central location for messages and information. Local residents mingled with miners who ventured from as far away as Wheeler Junction (now Copper Mountain) and ranchers from Dickey and Bill's Ranch. Adding to its significance, the post office/general store served also as the town commons, where people gathered to discuss recent happenings as they waited for the mail to arrive. There was no formal church in Frisco until the 1940s, so services were often held in the old Town Hall, which still stands and is now being used as a preschool. At some point in his ownership, Wildhack erected a two-story barn on the property that included an ice house/chicken house, using materials from nearby Admiral Mine. A blacksmith shop operated in the bottom half of the barn and remains of the forge still exist. In the next 10 years, the 1930s, tourist cabins were built on the property by another owner, Guy Cannam. The exterior of the cabins remain unaltered and still stand on Helen's property today.

During World War II, soldiers from Camp Hale's training facility would socialize across the street at the Chamberlain Café.

Helen Foote
and her brother,
Kelly White,
who lives
in the house
behind her's.

Helen Foote
in the part of
her house
that used to be
the Frisco Post Office.
P.O. boxes are visible
behind her.

The postmaster, a job held by Mary Ruth from 1942 to 1947, was given the difficult task of notifying families of the war dead or missing. Then in the happier days of the 1950s, a clock lighted by neon lights was placed on the front of the general store in its original place, however, it is now without neon lighting.

As its new owners, Helen, Bob and Nonnie spent two furious weeks cleaning and painting the general store, which they reopened as "Foote's Rest," and the four log cabins were cleaned and furnished as soon as possible. Bob became the postmaster in 1947 and served until 1965. In 1966, the post office was moved to a larger building on the corner of Fourth and Granite streets. In 1958, Helen accepted a new challenge of teaching home economics to junior high and high school students and was credited with the opening of the first home economics department at Breckenridge High School, now the present Colorado Mountain College building. Later, a new high school was built in Frisco. She retired from teaching in 1980.

On two separate, yet equally brief debuts, Helen and Bob attempted skiing, as the sport was gaining popularity in the County. Helen strapped on her skis, but ended up "splatting" on Fifth Street while she was practicing. Her husband, after deciding he was going to try skiing, ended up backing his 1930 Chevrolet pickup "Whoopee" into the bank with the skis sticking out the back and snapped them in half. He never went again. Their children took lessons and learned, however, at a special instructional facility in Frisco.

Meanwhile, she and Bob ran a thriving business and watched the community grow from their central Frisco location. "Customers began buying gasoline from our hand pump and tourists rented the cabins for one night or one week at a time," Helen recalled. "Some would even make reservations to return the following summer. If they were lucky enough to catch some fish during their stay, then they'd be sure to come back the next year. We met a lot of neat friends that way." The store closed in 1961 and Bob died in 1973. Three of their four children took up residence in surrounding towns while one son moved to California.

Today, Helen continues to live at 510 Main Street, which still has the original window panes, store display cases and the post office window and boxes. The original soft pine of the flooring creaks as if to share memories of days gone by. In 1984, Helen's home was placed on the National Registry of Historic Places. The east wing remains intact and serves as a museum for her and her family to enjoy, smiling back at the fun they've had watching Summit County grow and change.

❄

Freda Langell Nieters

"No one thought I even knew how to stop on skis.
I didn't do it very often."

— *Freda Langell Nieters on trying out for a ski school position at Keystone*

Freda (Opdahl) Langell Nieters was born with her skis on. Growing up in Norway in the same neighborhood as the great legend Stein Eriksen, skiing was her transportation as well as her pastime. Skiing has remained her lifelong passion. Today, after instructing for nearly 30 years in the United States, Freda boasts about her "beautiful office" on the majestic slopes of Keystone Resort.

Freda became a ski instructor and began teaching at Keystone on its November 1970 opening day. With most of the other Keystone instructors 20-something males, Freda needed to make a statement. She showed up in a yellow coat over green pants tucked into red patent-leather buckle boots. Resembling a human traffic light, she completed the outfit with a fur hat topped by a pompom as an exclamation point. Freda got noticed.

Yet they knew nothing of her race background. "No one thought I even knew how to stop on skis," she says. "I didn't do it very often." And Freda hasn't stopped since. Three decades of living in Summit County and 40,000 ski lessons later, she hasn't quit being a booster to her ski clients, friends and family.

Freda, who skied to and from school as a young girl and then as a teenager with the Norwegian National Ski Team (before a knee injury crushed Olympic hopes), is a born encourager. Her ability to create an atmosphere for success helped achieve a family triumph. Her daughter Ingrid Langell Butts, a former member of the U.S. Cross-country Ski Team, is a three-time Olympian participating in Winter Games at Calgary, Albertville and (apropos) Lillehammer, Norway. "I was there to cheer her on, waving two flags and clutching a box of Kleenex," Freda says. "It was a family dream come true."

"I try to share the spirit and beauty of the mountains with my students. Skiing is more than making turns."

Helping skiers' dreams come true remains Freda's forte. She treasures a memory of a weak skier on the Keystone beginner runs. Though the woman's progress was lackluster, Freda sensed she needed a breakthrough. "I gambled and took her to the top of Keystone Mountain. She lacked the skill so I skied backwards, holding on to steady her."

To Freda's surprise, the woman began to weep, not in frustration, but in joy. She confessed to Freda that, having once been a skier, she had suffered paralysis and was never expected to walk – much less ski – the panoramic Keystone summit again. "I try to share the spirit and beauty of the mountains with my students," Freda says. "Skiing is more than making turns."

Freda Langell Nieters at age 3 in Norway.

Freda Langell Nieters in Oslo at age 6 in national dress on the occasion of Norwegian Independence Day.

Freda's refusal to settle for the mediocre sets the stage for her achievements, not only the Norwegian Olympic squad but a long list: 1995 National Ski Instructor of the Year, listed in *Skiing* magazine's top 100 ski instructors; Professional Ski Instructors of America chief examiner in cross-country skiing; Colorado River raft guide; Ride the Rockies bicyclist; Summit High School race coach; Ski for Light participant; avid hiker, tennis coach and player; mother of five and grandmother of two.

Freda jumps feet first into these activities because she remains unruffled by fear of failure. She values the process of reaching the goal and accepts the outcome. Her philosophy: "Be productive, no matter what you do. Set your goal, be aware of the sacrifices. But learn to enjoy the journey, even if you don't meet that high goal. In school, skiing or life in general, learn to get up after you fall."

Freda has personally experienced rising after a fall. Grief struck her happy Summit County family when her eldest daughter, Astrid, was killed in an Alaskan plane crash. One year later, her second daughter, Karin, died in a tragic car crash as the recovering family prepared for her wedding. "Before this I was a self-reliant competitor. But without God, I wouldn't have overcome these losses. Before this, God was there when I had time. Now God is there all the time."

> *"Teaching technique is just a small part of teaching skiing.*
> *To me, teaching is also enabling students to learn*
> *to really enjoy the experience of being outside."*

The recipient of one of Freda's practical jokes would never suspect such sadness in her past. Each year on April Fool's Day, she poses as a ski student seeking a private lesson with one of her ski school colleagues. Disguised as a pink-suited, Tina Turner-wigged snow bunny or an Olga-from-Eastern-Europe in lumpy knickers and on wooden skis, she proceeds to pull off a stunt that challenges the instructor's ability to cope.

Freda's third daughter, Lisa, has a little girl named Whitney who plays with her prankish grandmother, Freda. In fact Lisa recently remarked to young Whitney, "You are lucky to have a grandmother your own age." As if in retaliation, nature seems to play pranks on Freda. One summer afternoon in the Dillon Valley home she was operating as a bed and breakfast, Freda removed the last tray of fragrant chocolate chip cookies from her oven. She decided to take a nice nap while the cookies cooled. Later she awoke to the sounds of a noisy guest rummaging in her kitchen, probably sneaking her cookies. Freda emerged irritated from her "den" to find a large bear devouring the treats.

Freda Langell Nieters
with some of Freda's Flying
Fossils at Keystone in 1999.

Freda Langell Nieters skiing with Freda's Flying Fossils
at Keystone in 1999.

No wonder the bed and breakfast was called "Freddie Bear's" and Freda now answers to the same name, sometimes shortened to "F.B." F.B. has always led a simple life. She's not the type for make-up or flashy cars. When she arrived from Oslo at the University of New Hampshire to begin her freshman year, she carried one "Mary Poppins" suitcase and a homemade ski bag. "My roommate," she says, "arrived with daddy and a U-Haul."

Ski students, tennis pals and hiking companions respond to Freda's simplicity. On a recent trek across a slippery cornice above Hoosier Pass, she took the hand of a frightened hiker. She does that with shaky ski students sometimes and the quiet gesture builds confidence.

Freda points out the many people who have helped her. Max and Edna Dercum, the ski legend couple who founded Arapahoe Basin and Keystone, raced with Freda in the Masters Alpine Competition and encouraged Freda and her family to move to Summit County. Employees of Keystone and its then-owner Ralston Purina Company enabled Ingrid to train for the Olympics with fundraisers and contributions. Ingrid's three-time Olympic success stands as Freda's peak life experience. "After the tragedies, our crumbled family reunited with happiness at these big events," Freda says.

Today Freda uses her resources to coach skiers and instructors, this time the famous "Flying Fossils," a group she founded at Keystone. These instructors, age 50 and older, participate in Freda's clinics under her training or that of top-notch outside clinicians. The Fossils are known for their strong people skills.

It is through the people she meets and works with – their experience of the mountain beauty and their delight in feeling competent on skis – that is Freda's reward for teaching and coaching. While living in Summit County, she has seized upon alpine sports as a way to help others live their lives as fully as she lives her own. Freda added, "Teaching technique is just a small part of teaching skiing. To me, teaching is also enabling students to learn to really enjoy the experience of being outside."

Many years after making a colorful statement on opening day, Freda is still getting noticed. Keystone recently named a run after their longtime instructor and her supportive style of teaching. It's called "Freda's Way."

❄

Howard Giberson

"I guess that if they hadn't put that road (I-70) in, I'd still be feeding cattle."

—Howard Giberson on the ongoing growth of Summit County

When Howard Giberson and his sister Edith Mary "Sue" Chamberlain were recently named Summit County Pioneers of the Year, Howard quietly accepted the honor. Born and raised on the same ranch in Summit County he owns today, Howard may not see himself as a modern-day pioneer. However, prevailing through the many economic, population and landscape changes has more than justified the title bestowed on him. During World War II, many young people left the county, but Howard stayed on the ranch. To Howard, Summit County has always been home.

"I can't remember not working because I was always on the ranch," said Howard with a shrug. He grew up on his parents' 320-acre ranch with only two neighbors in sight. When he married, he took over the ranch from his father and he and his wife, Lura Belle, added another 400 acres to the homestead. Today, the ranch has been reduced to 188 acres of pastureland at the foot of Buffalo Mountain with two cows and one horse. Approximately 160 acres of that land will forever be protected from future development thanks to a conservation easement he contributed to the Continental Divide Land Trust.

When the weather permitted, Howard, his two brothers and sister would ride horses to school. In the colder months, they drove a horse and sled to school. Their first family car was a Model T. Then his father bought a Stevens Touring car and later, when the boys began driving to Breckenridge for high school, they had a 1927 Buick with a rumble seat. Howard laughed and said, "Boy, we could really make dust fly."

---

*"I can't remember not working because
I was always on the ranch."*

Like an explorer born too late, Howard has covered nearly every inch of the surrounding forest, fields and creeks. Water would run through Howard's property from a lake up the canyon to a mine called the Royal Buffalo Placer near Silverthorne. He loved hiking into the backcountry and fly-fishing in Willow Lakes. When he was younger, Howard also enjoyed hunting. He would shoot rabbits, skin them and hang them up to freeze outside in the winter until he needed them. On various outings over the years he has spotted all sorts of wildlife tracks, such as bear, mountain lion and deer.

There were often many social gatherings and dances in Summit County during the first half of the century. It was attending one of those dances in Frisco back in 1936 that Howard caught his first glimpse of Lura Belle. Her mother had been there the year before to visit a friend who owned the Ophir Lodge on Bill's Ranch, which prompted Lura Belle to visit. Bill Thomas, the owner of Bill's Ranch, introduced Lura Belle and her friend to Howard and one of his friends. The match

Howard Giberson and wife, Lura Belle, about 1938.

Howard Giberson and burro, Blue, about 1920.

Sign at the entrance to
Howard Giberson's ranch.

Ranch buildings where Howard
and Lura Belle lived from 1937-1939.

was successful as Howard ended up marrying Lura Belle and and the two friends married as well. In 1992, just two months after their 55th wedding anniversary, Lura Belle passed away.

Howard and Lura Belle had taken over the ranching responsibilities from his father since his other two brothers didn't seem interested. She and Howard had no children to help out with the chores, so Lura Belle learned to drive a tractor and worked alongside Howard as a team. From 1937 to 1939, while the young couple resided in the rustic cabin, Lura Belle would also go out in the evening and catch three fish for dinner from Meadow Creek — two for Howard and one for herself. To earn some extra money, Howard worked on the construction crew assigned to open Loveland Pass in 1940. Then as the years passed and the County continued to grow, Lake Dillon was built and I-70 cut through his land. Howard began to cut back on the number of cattle he ran, because it became too difficult to raise 90 head of cattle, half of them calves, as he had most of his life, on less pasture.

> *"We would sit around the campfire every night just telling stories and laughing. It was a good time."*

For the past 23 years, Howard has ridden horses with a group of doctors, lawyers, surveyors and other professionals that called themselves the "Roundup Riders of the Rockies." "After riding once a year on journeys that took us from Wyoming to New Mexico, strong friendships developed," Howard said. It was an all-male group that enjoyed the camaraderie on horseback. Their 100-mile a week rides would be broken up by fun entertainers and horse shows. During that time, Howard rode two different horses, Dolly and Ginger.

"There were a lot of really good fellas on those trips," he recalled. "We would sit around the campfire every night just telling stories and laughing. It was a good time."

In the early days, there was no alpine skiing in Summit County. Instead, everyone participated in jumping and cross-country. Howard's first skis were four feet long with pieces of leather to strap them on. His leather work boots doubled as his ski boots. While the cost was prohibitive to own the new technology, he remembers the transformation in ski equipment over the years. He skied actively throughout the 30s until he twisted his ankle. He then began competing in cross-country ski races and has a wall full of ribbons to show off his accomplishments.

Howard continues the physical labor of working outside because he believes it is "good for him." He admitted, "I guess that if they hadn't put that road (I-70) in, I'd still be feeding cattle." Thinking back on the then and now, he says, "I feel satisfied with the life I've lived — living and ranching. Even though it was a lot of hard work, it was pretty satisfying."

Jim Bowden

"It just touched my heart. I saw these mountains and I felt the power and the energy. It was just all there for me."

—Jim Bowden on coming to Summit County

For Jim Bowden, taking risks was as much a part of everyday life as waking up in the morning. To him, living in the mountains became a combination of love and testing limits.

"We were involved in a game, and in my way of thinking, it was a game of death. People died playing this game. The game was, 'Who's going to get the steep gullies or the beaver gullies open first. Who's going to get the first set of tracks in the beavers.' It went on for 19 years and during that time six people died," Jim said. "Risk-taking here was a way of life."

At age 26, three things happened to Jim Bowden that radically altered the course of his life. First, he lost his job as a physical education teacher for skipping a day of work to go skiing. Second, he and his wife divorced. Third, his grandfather died. With all of these things happening within a six-month period, Jim decided it was time to leave Buffalo, New York and start fresh. So he jumped into his '66 Volkswagon with $60 and a lunch packed by his mother and headed west. That lunch lasted all the way to Keystone.

Jim grew up in North Tanawanda, New York, right on the Niagara River and the Erie Canal. In 1963, he earned his bachelor's degree in education from New York State University while playing football on scholarship for former NFL coach Buddy Ryan. That same year he also earned his Professional Ski Instructors of America certification. He was first introduced to the sport in 1952 wearing a pair of old hand-carved skis that his father gave him. It was 1968 when Jim left the East Coast and just briefly passed through Summit County on his way to Aspen to attend the Eighth Interski, which was a gathering for skiing nations from around the world to get together and compare teaching techniques. In those days, he recalls not even having enough money to buy a lift ticket, but since no one really checked anyway, it was easy to ride the lift without one.

To add to his "self discovery" period of life, Jim moved to Laguna Beach, California to take up surfing for awhile until the mountains beckoned him to return. "It just touched my heart," said Jim. "I saw these mountains and I felt the power and the energy. It was just all there for me. I felt like this is where my heart belonged and I really wanted to come and be part of this life." He worked as an independent ski instructor for two years in Aspen before moving to Summit County in 1969 to get involved on the ground floor of a new ski area that was just opening. That ski resort was Keystone. He became acquainted with Max Dercum and son Rolf who hired him on the spot to teach skiing. Ski Tip Lodge in Keystone, owned and operated by the Dercums in those days, was the cultural hub of the skiing community. This is where people gathered to discuss technique and, Jim added with a smile, to socialize. In those days, there was about a 50-to-1 men-to-women ratio. People would also go to hear rock-n-roll at the Old Dillon Inn and country music at The Mint, where fights always seemed to break out among miners, cowboys and hippies. "Wow," Jim remembers thinking, "this really is the wild West!"

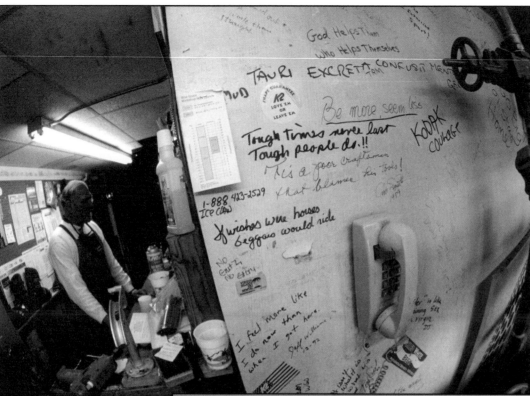

Quotes on the wall in Jim Bowden's ski repair shop.

Jim Bowden on Loveland Pass in search of summer skiing.

While he was instructing, he worked a number of odd jobs — from plumbing, to construction, to building ski lifts — in order to support himself. "Those were hard days," he remembers. "There was not much money, but I was just experiencing all these different things. I guess I never thought of us as ski bums because everybody worked like hell. Most of us had to be strong enough to ski all day and then be able to do a decent night's work in order to afford our lifestyle."

Jim worked on the construction crew building the Keystone Lodge from May through November for $94 a week. Then they would be laid off in November and ski all winter long until they resumed work the following May. "On $94 a week, you could afford a ski pass, a place to live, food and beer, but that was about it," said Jim.

Jim also built lifts for Heron Poma in the early '70s on Copper Mountain as well as at Keystone and Steamboat. Keystone was the first mountain to use helicopters in place of building roads to each tower site. After two years of skiing, Jim took a job in product development with Head Skis in Boulder. He traveled to a different ski area every week for a seasonal promotion of the skis and to host demo days at the resorts.

"I just decided that I wasn't going to teach skiing anymore. I really wanted to get out on the mountains, hike, climb and ski every peak that I could see around here," said Jim.

During a 10-year span from 1973 to 1983, Jim embarked on his death-defying decade of risk-taking and one-up-manship among his cronies. They were continually warned of the hazards of skiing out of bounds, but he admits that big egos were at work when it came to making some of these dangerous decisions. They set out to challenge their skiing skills and abilities of accessing avalanche-prone zones. "The good skiers were climbing and taking risks. We were just following our love. Because we loved it so much, I guess we thought it was worth the risk."

"The good skiers were climbing and taking risks. We were just following our love. Because we loved it so much, I guess we thought it was worth the risk."

One of his good friends Bill Harris tore his Achilles' tendon in an avalanche while filming a movie called "Powder Hounds" back in the Chihuahua Gulch. Jim remembers Bill saying, "When the camera turns on, the I.Q. drops to zero." Jim also starred in many Warren Miller movies performing outrageous stunts. Looking back, he said, his friends, in pursuit of the 'hedonistic powder pleasure,' needed little coaxing to do things most considered life threatening. "I've jumped off a cliff for Polio. I've jumped off a cliff for Muscular Dystrophy. I've even jumped off a cliff for Coors Beer." Even with his experience as a National Avalanche School graduate, Jim acknowledged that daily risk-taking would inevitably result in someone screwing up.

Jim Bowden on Dave's Wave near Loveland Pass.
Photo by Bruce Schaeffer

Jim Bowden, the Ski Doctor.
Photo by Hank Parker

Indeed a tragedy did occur — an avalanche on Peak 7 at Breckenridge Ski Resort that claimed several lives in 1987. The accident spurred a meeting between the Summit County ski areas and Woody Woodrow, the Forest Service Supervisor, at the Holiday Inn Summit in Frisco. The meeting was closed to the skiing public and a decision was made to close the extreme terrain adjacent to lift serviced ski area terrain and at Arapahoe Basin, a mountain known for its challenging slopes. A double perimeter rope signaled that certain territory was off-limits to the public. An outcry from the local skiers and backcountry travelers was heard. Jim took immediate action by calling Jim Gregg of the United States Forest Service in Silverthorne as well as the NBC news team covering the Breckenridge avalanche. He also called his lawyer, Jim Onlott in Denver, to discuss the Skier Safety Act of 1979. "With four of my friends and the NBC camera crew, I decided to ski through the closure at Arapahoe Basin," said Jim. "My basic premise for this act of defiance was that the ski area did not have the right to block access to Forest Service Land." It turned out he was right and a gate was installed at Arapahoe Basin atop the Norway lift. The gate can only be legally closed by the USFS and it is still there today.

During the summer months, he skateboarded on specially designed skateboards to refine his balance. He built and sold more than 200 skateboards in the late 1970s. They had a competitive league and people came from all over the country to race in Summit County. He remembers being clocked skating down Loveland Pass going 72 miles per hour and competed in another race down Swan Mountain Road for $10,000 and another down Hoosier Pass. The sheriff was always after him for skateboarding. "I'm not saying it was sane," Jim said. "There was some real insanity going on here." In the end, he admitted that he just might have been lucky. Jim said, "I guess if I had to choose between luck and skill, I'd pick luck."

A clever "Ski the Summit" ad campaign ran in a local newspaper in the mid-1970s, promoting area tourism by proclaiming that "the doctor is in." (See photo opposite page.) From then on, Jim became known as the "Ski Doctor," using his many years of experience and expertise to repair ski equipment in his Frisco Holiday Inn ski repair shop. However, for Jim, skiing has always been much more than his livelihood. It has been like a drug for his soul. Today, the doctor is still in. Those who visit him will get more than a fresh tune or new wax. They may get a taste of the glory days from a legend in his own time. Jim Bowden is a man who carved fresh tracks not only on the new fallen snow, but in his fearless efforts to confront the previously unexplored, trying stunts never before attempted. As a cure to prevent the body from ever growing bored or passionless, Jim might advise a constant dose of adrenaline. Then take two runs and call him in the morning.

❄

Bernie and Linda McMenamy

"Somebody said, 'Who are you up here with?' and I said, 'I don't know. His name (McMenamy) sounds like a flower.' I didn't even know what his last name was, but he was on the ski patrol so he was sort of hot stuff."

—*Linda McMenamy on her first skiing date with Bernie in 1958 at Winter Park*

There is a call – one that is so clear and so wild that it cannot be denied. It is the call of the mountains. Bernie McMenamy paid heed to the message that beckoned him nearly 53 years ago to move to higher altitudes, where a life full of strange new experiences was awaiting.

A Colorado native born in Denver, Bernie arrived in 1947 at the Climax mine near Leadville at age 17. There wasn't a lot of action in Summit County, especially in Breckenridge, which at that time only had about 200 or 300 residents. He lived in what was probably one of the last boarding houses for miners, working in the summers and over Christmas holidays for the next few years. Although they didn't know each other yet, Linda was also a second-generation Coloradan, living in Colorado Springs.

"My father thought I was out of my mind for skiing," Bernie said. His father, who came to Denver in 1882, worked as a miner at Camp Bird Mine in Ouray for several years where he skied merely as a means of transportation from the mine to town. He had once told Bernie about a tragic avalanche accident near Ouray in 1905 that left several people dead, and simply couldn't comprehend why anyone would pursue the sport for pleasure. Before there was ski slope grooming, there was a practice skiers referred to as "filling your sitzmark." Translated, this meant that skiers were expected to pack snow in holes caused by falling, in an effort to prevent other skiers from falling.

Following his experience at Climax, Bernie worked on his education in Denver and attended Regis High School and College. While there, Bernie began skiing at Winter Park. Possessing no modern grooming equipment, Winter Park offered a free lift ticket for volunteers who ski-packed for two hours in the morning. Ski area manager Steve Bradley would later engineer the first grooming apparatus, the Bradley Packer, designed to be dragged behind a skier to groom the snow. It was an extremely dangerous device, however, because it was so difficult to control the speed going down a hill. Bernie added that if the operator hit a sharp bump, it nearly knocked the wind out of him. For Bernie, the desire to ski was so intense during those years that even when he and his friends didn't have much money for lift tickets, they would still find a way to go. They would use cars to drive to the top of both Loveland and Berthoud passes, ski down and a car would be at the bottom to take them back to the top again. It became a ritual to ski Hell's Half Acre and the Eleven Mile Trail to Winter Park from the top of Berthoud in the morning, and the Hoop Creek Trail down to Empire in the evenings.

Bernie then joined the Denver Metro Ski Patrol (National Ski Patrol), which served Arapahoe Basin, Winter Park, Berthoud Pass and Loveland Pass ski areas. As a patroller, he taught avalanche safety and first aid. A former competitive skier from Regis University, Bernie patrolled until 1951 when he joined the Navy and spent two years in Guam.

When he completed his tour of duty, Bernie returned to the state he loved and worked as a heating and air conditioning engineer and contractor. It wasn't long, however, before the mountains were summoning him again. This time he found himself in Aspen.

The Bergenhof Restaurant at Breckenridge in the 1960s.

Tara, Linda and Keli
McMenamy in 1971.

Tara, Linda and Keli
McMenamy in 1999.

"When I went to Aspen to join the ski patrol," Bernie recalled, "I had a pair of skis, a suitcase and about $5,000 of debt."

The aprés ski scene had a different flavor than it does today. Most skiers went directly from the slopes to the bars rather than going back to their condos and showering or napping. "We were lucky if we even got dinner," Linda recalled. "Usually we walked into bars still wearing our ski clothes and just partied." It was in 1957 at a bar owned by Ski Hall of Famer Steve Knowlton called the Golden Horn that Linda first saw Bernie in the Golden Horn Floor Show. That "glance across a crowded room" that only seems to happen on Hollywood sets must have made quite an impression on Linda. Even though she and Bernie didn't officially meet until the following year when they lived in the same apartment house in Denver. On February 1, they went skiing for their first official date and four days later they got engaged. They did, however, wait until after Lent to get married on April 12, 1958.

Linda laughs when she retells the story of that first date with Bernie. "Somebody asked, 'Who are you here with?' and I said, 'I don't know. His name (McMenamy) sounds like a flower.' I didn't even know what his last name was. But he was on the ski patrol, so he was sort of hot stuff."

Once they were married and living in Denver, Bernie accepted an assignment to survey 480 acres on the south edge of Breckenridge for a friend. He was offered an opportunity to buy the three mining claims for $15,000, but didn't have the money then. At that time, there were no plans for a ski area to be built, but the Dillon Dam was imminent so he assumed the land would eventually appreciate. During the next three years, until 1960, principals of Rounds and Porter Lumber Company of Wichita, Kansas came to town and started buying up properties. In total, the Kansas company purchased approximately 5,500 acres and several buildings in Breckenridge, many of them for the defaulted taxes owed. In exchange for his surveying efforts, which took place over six weekends, Bernie received 12 acres. He eventually sold that land for $40,000.

"When I went to Aspen to join the ski patrol, I had a pair of skis, a suitcase and about $5,000 of debt."

While the fondness for the more tranquil mountain lifestyle remained imbedded in their souls, the McMenamys, a skiing family, waited another 10 years before they made the decision to move to Breckenridge. Self-declared pioneers, Bernie and Linda were in search of a change of pace from city life. In 1971, they convinced their three children to move with grand promises of a better life in Summit County. They told their son that he would be able to skate up and down the Blue River like Hans Brinker, the youngest daughter that she would be able to fish out the back window of their newly acquired barn with the creek running just behind, and their middle daughter that she would own a horse. The middle daughter is the only one that saw her wish realized. With everyone's wish lists written up, they sold their larger Denver home, and bought the corner of Watson and Main Street, Breckenridge. The ski area, now owned by Aspen Ski Corp., was destined to expand. With many years of renovation and a lot of tender loving care, Bernie and Linda still have the same address, although they now live in what was once the barn and the Near Gnu second-hand store. Their former residence has become the Ready, Paint, Fire pottery painting shop.

Breckenridge residents at the town park during the 1976 Bicentennial celebration. Maureen Nicholls is the fifth from the left, standing. Linda McMenamy is the eighth from the left, standing in the back row.

Linda and Bernie McMenamy in 1976 at the Breckenridge Town Party celebrating the Bicentennial.

"When we first came to Breckenridge, probably 50% of the lots on Main Street were empty," recalled Bernie. "I was on the Town Council then and we were just crying for someone to come and build something here." He explained how their move to Breckenridge had been so sudden. "Linda and the children really had a lot of courage to go along with all this nonsense. It was pretty lonesome here. Just a very quiet town in those days. The town in 1971 was rather shabby, and the County had few services. Grocery shopping and shopping for supplies was mostly done in Leadville over Fremont Pass or Denver over Loveland Pass."

When they first planned their move, Bernie fully expected to continue to operate a heating and plumbing business. Instead, he tended bar at the old Breckenridge Inn for three months before Linda and the children joined him at the end of their school year. In the meantime, he applied for a position on the ski patrol and soon received a call to work at the ski area. During the summer months, Bernie worked on the trail maintenance crew and eventually ran the lift crews during the following winter months. One October, he was given the insidious task of building a new t-bar during the winter, which was successfully completed, but not without plenty of hardship and challenges. He also was mountain manager for six years.

From the moment he arrived in town, Bernie took an active role in town government and various other organizations. Perhaps the role that put him in the spotlight was serving as mayor of Breckenridge from 1978 to 1982. He also served on the Town Council for 14 years, and on the Red, White and Blue Fire Board and Breckenridge Sanitation District Board.

"The fire department in the early 1970s was not all it should be." he admitted. "They had a big red truck, a little red truck and a jeep. The water tank in the little red truck didn't have any baffles, so if you turned a corner going more than 15 miles per hour, the water would slosh and nearly turn over the truck!" Bernie distinctly remembers that whenever the bell would ring for the volunteers everybody would head for the firehouse because they all wanted to drive the truck.

The keys were always left in the ignition of the fire truck, as Breckenridge was such a small, trusting place. As a joke, kids would sometimes climb in and turn on the key so the battery would go dead. One time they actually had to tow the truck behind a Jeep to get to a fire because the battery was dead. Weekends were probably the most chaotic. On Saturday nights, everybody would rush to fire calls which took place on a regular basis. "The drunkest guys were the most forward so they would get at the front end of the hose and squirt just about everything but the fire." Shrugging and shaking his head, Bernie said, "What can I say? The fire department was just dangerous." In 1974, the Town made concerted efforts to correct the fire department's tarnished reputation by finally forming a fire district, appointing a paid fire chief, building new fire houses and buying new equipment. Many other quality improvements were made to turn it into the outstanding professional and volunteer organization it is now.

Today, with their children grown, Bernie and Linda continue to enjoy the simple pleasures of life in Summit County. The coziness of their home full of historical memorabilia and old pictures gives visitors a sense that sometimes you just have to follow your heart. The warm feelings the McMenamys have found in their years in Breckenridge are for a caring community, good and loyal friends and a sense of belonging.

❄

Joe Bailey

"Some days if we got a dozen people buying tickets to ski, it was a good day."

—Joe Bailey on the early days at Arapahoe Basin

Arriving in Dillon in 1948 with little more than his skis, Joe "Tink" Bailey joined a band of rugged outdoorsmen that some called true Arapahoe people. Their experiences were legendary because of the hardships and sacrifices they endured for the sake of the carefree lifestyle they desired in Summit County.

"We were all paupers," said Joe. "We all chose an entirely different lifestyle than most people. We had to give up any big dreams we might have had to live this way." However, whereas the money may have been lacking, the scenery, the skiing and the laughter were in great abundance. Joe recalled the president of Shell Oil, Co., after enjoying himself at one of their typical Saturday night barbecues, saying, "I sure wish I had enough money to live like you boys do!"

"We'd go to bed some Saturday nights and wake up in the morning to find some 18 people sleeping on the floor, in the kitchen or wherever."

Joe grew up in New England and competed on the Middlebury College ski team in Vermont. With a deep passion for the outdoors, Joe was drawn to Colorado for the mountains and by the coaxing of his two brothers who had already paved the way. All three settled at Arapahoe Basin and lived in a small, three-room cabin on Route 6 in the old town of Dillon. With no indoor plumbing, they would haul 10-gallon milk cans full of water from a spring on Loveland Pass each day on their way to and from Arapahoe Basin. In the summer, they often collected their water from the Conoco Station in the center of town. Once a week they would buy a shower at the Heart of the Rockies Cabin Camp in Dillon for $.50, unless they had female guests visiting, in which case they would make an extra trip to clean up.

Ski Tip Lodge was the only lodge in the county for a long time. It attracted many overnight guests from Denver and the Front Range who came up to go skiing. For the locals, Ski Tip served as a forum for any meetings, such as ski school gatherings. It also quickly became the place to be on Saturday nights, New Year's Eve or any other social occasion. One of the main attractions for the young bachelors was Edna Dercum's kitchen staff, which usually included college women and a house full of other ski bums. To "compete" with the Ski Tip, Joe and his brothers often allowed friends from the University of Colorado to crash at their cabin they fondly called the "Ski Boot Inn," even though they never actually collected any money.

"We'd go to bed some Saturday nights and wake up in the morning to find some 18 people sleeping on the floor, in the kitchen or wherever," Joe said. Eventually Joe's brother bought a house in Dillon and the three moved out of the cabin to share the house.

Far left is Dick Bailey, Joe's younger brother.
Joe Bailey is fourth from the left, standing.
Arapahoe Basin ski school circa 1960.

The early days of Arapahoe Basin circa 1948.

Joe Bailey racing at Big Bromley in 1947.

When Joe first arrived just before the 1950s, skiing was just getting started. Grooming consisted of an individual in skis sidestepping to pack down snow on the slope. It was considered a sport for the "rugged type" and climbing and backcountry skiing were just a way of life in those days. He and his brothers worked as ski instructors at Arapahoe Basin during the day and often journeyed to Climax for night skiing after hours. Joe said Climax was "about as rugged as you could get." To Joe, it all just felt so natural. "We were outdoor people, and if you're an outdoor person, this was the place to be," he said.

"We were outdoor people,
and if you're an outdoor person,
this was the place to be."

"Particularly in spring, we would be especially active and often pushed ourselves to see how many sports we could do in one day. We'd ski in the morning, then kayak and then maybe have a ballgame in the afternoon." Working outdoors and spending his days on the mountain seeped into Joe's soul, and he instructed for 18 years before taking his vast teaching experience to Keystone in 1969. Joe also made an instrumental impact on the amputee ski program at Arapahoe Basin while teaching there.

On many a Saturday night, Joe and his friends enjoyed attending dances at Slate Creek Hall. Sometimes the ranchers would invite them to go horseback riding in the Gore Range. Through these contacts, Joe thought it was important to introduce skiing to the ranch children and get them interested in the sport. With ranching on the decline and the ski business on the rise, he thought it might be a good way to keep the younger ranching generation in the County. Serving as the superintendent of schools, Joe's brother started a ski program for the school children.

An adventurous spirit pushed Joe and others to explore an abundance of unexplored terrain. They ventured into the Gore Range quite often, but even skiing Arapahoe Basin required some climbing in those days. "There was never a worry about finding fresh tracks," Joe said. "Some days, if we sold a dozen lift tickets it was a good day." No one had any qualms about skiing moguls either, it was just part of the skiing experience. Each day there was an endless source of deep powder skiing. "We skied everywhere, but at the proper time. I don't know if we were better educated, but we sure knew what an avalanche slope was and we stayed off of them. A lot of these places that people are skiing today we didn't ski until spring when the snow sets up," he said. "We'd ski Little Professor every Easter morning. We'd go up there and have a beer and hold our own personal sunrise service, then ski down."

Joe went off the old jump in Dillon (now under water) shortly after arriving in Summit County. He spent the entire day

Joe Bailey at a cross-country ski race
in Sun Valley in 1948.

Joe "Tink" Bailey
at Keystone
in 1999.

Joe Bailey's 1956/57 Bogner ski school parka
and patch, custom-made boots, skis and poles.

packing the fresh snow out wearing eight-foot jumping skis. Finally, braving his first attempt, Joe flew down the jump, soared into the air for about 100 feet and hit the landing. When his skis submarined into six feet of snow, Joe decided that jumping wasn't for him any more.

Once a month Joe and his brothers or friends drove over Loveland Pass to Denver for their shopping, or sometimes to the company store at Climax. For entertainment, they would go to a play or a concert while they were down on the Front Range.

One of their favorite things to do in Denver was to attend the premiere showing of a John Jay ski movie. For local nightlife, they mostly saved their energies for the slopes, but occasionally indulged in a night at the Gold Pan or the bowling alley once located on the south end of Breckenridge. For many years, the only barber in Summit County was in Breckenridge, so they had to drive from Dillon if they needed a haircut.

To continue in his life of skiing, hiking and high-altitude dwelling, Joe worked a number of odd jobs over the years. He pumped gas at a filling station, kept books for the Conoco gas station, sold real estate, worked for Public Service and served on a construction crew at Climax for a couple years, to name a few. Joe even worked on the ditch designed to divert water from the bottom of Loveland Pass to a hydro-electric plant, where the Silverthorne Fair Grounds are now located, before the Dillon Dam was built. He helped keep the ditch from freezing up in the winter so the water would continue flowing to the plant. As soon as the Lake was filled, Joe's brother, elected mayor of Dillon, gained the rights to run the marina at Dillon. Joe began teaching skiing in the winter and worked at the marina during the summer. His brother operated the marina for nearly 10 years. Joe's responsibilities included removing docks and the moorings that held the boats as winter approached.

"The lake brought on a whole new lifestyle," Joe explained. "Instead of being mountain people, we were lake people all of a sudden."

Today, living in Frisco, Joe likes to walk the long way to collect his mail, via Rainbow Lake and Masontown to the post office. Sometimes he visits Ophir Mountain where one of his brothers used to have mining claims or one of his favorite places on top of Peaks One, Two and Three. Wherever Joe goes or whatever he does, he takes that adventurous Arapahoe spirit and love of the mountains with him.

❄

Sue (Giberson) Chamberlain

"One time my mother kept track of how many extra people were at our house for meals.

There was almost always someone dropping by.

Everybody was always welcome to eat and we always found room for one more."

—*Sue (Giberson) Chamberlain on growing up on the ranch.*

Edith Mary "Sue" (Giberson) Chamberlain said, "We are a generation too late to remember many of the facts about life in Summit County." She is skeptical that all of life's modern conveniences and technological advances have made the world a better place.

Born and raised on a ranch that was located about halfway between Frisco and the old town of Dillon, Sue is from a family whose land is now covered by the water of Lake Dillon. Sue's father owned a cattle ranch and although they lived through the Great Depression, there was always enough food for everyone. They raised cows, pigs and chickens, and produced milk, butter and cheese. Aside from potatoes her father would buy from a farmer in the Lower Blue, they would pick up a few staples at the Dillon grocery store. "My mother did a lot of baking," she said. "Pies, cakes, cookies and bread."

"It seemed like my mother was always cooking.
But she never used a recipe.
Just a pinch of this and a pinch of that, all on a wood stove."

Until 1937, the C&S Railroad would bring shipments every day from Denver, on a route that would go to Como, over Boreas Pass, into Breckenridge, down to Dillon, Frisco and then on to Leadville. Sue's family shipped cattle to market in Denver on the same route.

Before Loveland Pass opened, the only way to drive to Denver was over Hoosier Pass or Berthoud Pass. "They didn't keep the roads open because there was no modern machinery like we have today to clear snow," Sue explained. "The C&S Railroad was crooked and slow, so *The Denver Post* would be a day late when it came by train. Once the train quit running, the roads were kept open more often and supplies began to be trucked up rather than arrive on the train."

As the only daughter with four older brothers, Sue had to endure much teasing and cajoling. Her fifth brother died when he was just a baby. For 11 years, Sue went to school in the old town of Dillon, but for her senior year, her parents rented an apartment in Denver and she attended North High School. The boys stayed at the ranch and finished high school in Breckenridge.

"It was the hardest thing I ever did," recalled Sue. With a class of 656 students it was a bit overwhelming for a girl from the mountains who didn't know anyone in the city or her way around Denver. "I was so homesick that I cried every night, but by the last semester, I was alright. I had become used to it by then."

Sue Chamberlain in 1944.

Sue Chamberlain and her horse, Bird, in 1934.

Sue described ranch life as non-stop hard work. Every family member knew to lend a hand and do his or her part, and no one slept until the work was complete. The boys would wake up early every morning to complete their chores of milking the cows, feeding the calves, pigs and chickens and mending fences. "Dad would always tell us to go to bed, because 5 o'clock comes early," remembered Sue. On the days that Sue helped milk the cows or worked in the hay fields, she too would be out of bed at dawn's earliest hour.

After graduation, Sue returned to the ranch for three years before attending nurse's training at St. Anthony's in Denver. She joined the Army Nurse Corps and spent some time at Camp Carson, now called Fort Carson, toward the end of World War II. After she was discharged from the army, she worked in Colorado Springs until September 1947, when she and Charles Chamberlain were married at the ranch. Living in Grand Junction for four years during which time they inherited license plate ZL-3, one of the oldest plates in the County, from Sue's father, they then moved back to Summit County. From 1951 to 1981, they lived in the log cabin that was once a café and later became the ReMax Real Estate office. She helped her husband run the Texaco Station next door. Their two daughters attended school in Frisco.

"When I stop and look back on things,
I can only think of how much fun we had.
I don't think about how times were hard,
because life was so much more simple then."

Sue reminisced about the days when the County was smaller and people got together more often for dances, card parties and pot lucks. Before the County became so populated, they knew everyone. It also seemed that there was an endless flow of visitors stopping by the ranch. There was a pond on the ranch where friends would come to ice skate. The boys would burn old tires on a camp fire on the side of the lake to grill burgers.

"One time my mother kept track of how many extra people were at our house for meals," said Sue. "There was almost always someone dropping by. Everybody was always welcome to eat and we always found room for one more."

Whenever anyone came by, there was always coffee, cake and pie to serve them. They had no modern conveniences such as indoor plumbing, electricity, telephone or running water, Sue recalls her mother often laden with buckets of water from

Sue Chamberlain in her World War II nurse's uniform with family photos.

their well to cook or do the wash. Before electricity, they first used kerosene, then gas, to light the rooms. At one point, the town of Frisco relied on electricity generated by the Excelsior mine during its operation.

"It seemed like my mother was always cooking," Sue said. "But she never used a recipe. Just a pinch of this and a pinch of that, all on a wood stove." It was usually late when Sue's family finished a meal, but they never missed an opportunity to gather around the stove and listen to stories.

"My mother was a good reader," Sue recalled. "We would pick out a book, and sit, wide-eyed, waiting for the next story. My favorite stories were mysteries." When her parents bought their first radio, the family started listening to programs such as "Amos and Andy" and "Fibber McGee and Molly" on one of the three stations. Sue's family later had one of the first televisions in Frisco and enjoyed watching the old westerns.

Of all the changes in Summit County over the years, Lake Dillon probably had the biggest geographical impact. It dramatically affected people who lived on the Blue between Old Dillon and Kremmling. The town of Dillon was moved and the cemetery, where two of Sue's brothers were buried, was relocated. For the Gibersons, the Lake meant losing their ranch to Denver's water supply as well as to the recreational pursuits of boating and fishing that interested the new generation.

"We were very content," smiled Sue. "Today, you have all these things that are supposed to make life easier and yet we still don't have as much time as we used to. When I stop and look back on things, I can only think of how much fun we had. I don't think about how times were hard, because life was so much more simple then."

Max and Edna Dercum

"I had to learn to turn or else I would have ended up in Italy."

—*Edna Dercum on learning to ski with Max while on their honeymoon*
at Jungfraujoch, Switzerland

American writer Katherine Anne Porter once said, "Adventure is something you seek for pleasure, or even for profit, like a gold rush or invading a country; . . . but experience is what really happens to you in the long run; the truth that finally overtakes you." For Max and Edna Dercum, it was their adventurous spirit that led them to the Colorado gold rush of 1942 – the year they moved to Summit County in search of the perfect ski mountain on which to hatch their dream. Their prospecting resulted in the birth of two world-class ski areas and more than 50 years of memories of their incredible experiences in the high country.

In 1941, Max made an exploratory trip to Colorado, from Pikes Peak to Aspen, from the Elk Mountains to the Front Range. Recalling how he first discovered Keystone, Max said, "I searched over a wide area, but I just didn't find a place that really caught my eye. I met Thor Groswold, who had a ski factory in Denver. He suggested Montezuma, the old mining area up the Snake River Valley west of Loveland Pass. And when I saw those endless slopes, I knew I'd found what I was searching for."

Edna agreed, adding, "We were so happy to find Colorado and all the freedom. People here took you at face value."

Max may say skiing was "in the genes." Even his mother continued to cross-country ski until she was 98 years old. He received his first pair of skis, a pair of Northlands, in 1917 at age 5. Growing up, Max read about the famous Norwegian skier Ehrling Strom in a mid-1920s Northlands' brochure and used the photos as examples of proper technique since there was really no one around to formally teach him. Years later, as an assistant professor of forestry at Pennsylvania State University, Max wanted to get involved in forest-based recreation. As a ski coach and competitive skier himself, skiing was the area that most appealed to him.

It was while he was in the Penn State Forestry School that Max first met Edna. She joined his ski club in Pennsylvania and joked that she was very happy to meet him, because now she could get free ski lessons. Actually, she said, it was the adventurous lifestyle he enjoyed that most attracted her. They celebrated their 62nd wedding anniversary in 1999.

Edna fondly remembers one of their first skiing excursions together on the Jungfraujoch, Switzerland and said, "I had to learn to turn or else I would have ended up in Italy!"

Evidently she was a good student, because Edna began to race in downhill events the first year she learned to ski. She remembers the popularity of ski racing in the 1930s, especially in the Eastern and Western parts of the United States. They wore seven-foot wooden skies with bear trap bindings and low-cut, leather lace-up boots. Some of the skis had metal edges, so skiers had to go home at night and tighten the screws that held them on because all the flexing that the ski did on the slopes would loosen them. Racers didn't wear helmets, and courses were usually boot-packed to a width of 15 to 20 feet, so skiers didn't want to veer off to the sides into the unpacked snow. Racers would start with the wave of a flag visible from the bottom and a timekeeper clicking his stopwatch. One of the first Olympic tryout races was to be held in Mt. Hood, Oregon. However, when war broke out, the 1940 Olympics were

Ski Tip Lodge circa 1948.

Max and Edna Dercum at
Arapahoe Basin in 1948.

canceled. Edna had been planning on competing since she had just placed in the California state championships in 1938. Max operated one of the first ski schools in the country in Stanislaus National Forest, California during a leave of absence from teaching.

With plans for a ski area brewing in the back of his mind, Max and Edna returned to Summit County after the war in 1945 with their 3-month-old son Rolf and 2-year-old daughter Sunni. They made their home in the rustic shelter of the Alhambra Cabin on Montezuma Road. In that cabin, Max and others drew up plans for Arapahoe Basin, one of Colorado's earliest ski areas, which opened in 1947. Among the planning group was Thor Groswold, notable Norwegian jumper, maker of the Groswold ski and father to Jerry Groswold, who later became long-time manager of Winter Park. Another contributor was Larry Jump, who had served with the 10th Mountain Division. Dick Durrance, another famous ski racer, also showed interest, along with a couple of others, in joining the elite group of five who eventually formed a small corporation. It cost $10 to register with the state, so each of them put up $2 and Arapahoe Basin was born.

Max described Arapahoe Basin as being "pretty primitive skiing." On weekends, they would attract 20 to 30 people to the mountain to use a rope tow and just a frame-like shelter for visitors to get out of the wind. In the second year, they were able to build a chair lift from midway to the top. It was constructed before the one connecting the bottom to the midway point, so skiers were hauled up by whatever means possible until the bottom lift was completed. During the first two years, there were only about 3,000 skiers per year. Later, as Colorado skiing began to gain popularity, Edna remembers the old Arapahoe Basin lodge burning down as skiers continued to drive in wanting to buy lift tickets. "Marny Jump was out there telling everyone that the mountain was closed, meanwhile, I was on the practice hill teaching beginners with burning ash blowing across the snow," Edna said.

"The first time I ever drew water from our well at Ski Tip, I pulled up a dead squirrel! I decided we couldn't drink that."

In 1941, Max and Edna purchased the old Black Homestead near Keystone and renamed it the Ski Tip Lodge. The old homestead dated back to the Homestead Act of 1862. Ski Tip was pretty primitive in those days with waxed chicken paper covering the windows to keep the snow from blowing in since there was no glass. "The first time I drew water from our well at Ski Tip, I pulled up a dead squirrel!" recalled Edna. "I decided we couldn't drink that."

Lodging at Ski Tip began with four rooms and a bathroom down the hall and "beavers for neighbors." Max and Edna continued to build additions as demand dictated. The Lodge, with its hewed timber walls, was a place for skiers to find fellowship and often a night's rest. It became an ongoing clean-up and remodel project in which many friends and guests participated. In 1952, they hired their first cook and charged $3.50 for a night's lodging, including breakfast and dinner served family style. Lunch wasn't

The Dercums with friends on the way up to ski
Peak 10 near Breckenridge in 1953.

Edna Dercum near the top of Peak 10
near Breckenridge in 1953.

Max Dercum doing rope tricks at Ski Tip in 1998.

offered because everyone, including the staff, wanted to get out and ski. Ski Tip's notoriety grew and soon the evenings were filled with music, story-telling and square dancing in the living room. It became Summit County's "place to be" as guests exchanged skiing techniques and a lot of laughter. One day, Edna remembers noticing that the guests had voluntarily changed the rates to $8.50 a night. She was worried that no one would come. Today, while no longer owned by Max and Edna, the allure of Ski Tip continues, reminiscent of skiing's rich history. The price tag, however, has changed over the years, with a night's accommodation during high season hovering around $130 a night, not including meals.

Among its famous visitors, Henry Fonda brought his wife, daughter and three cousins to Ski Tip for a pack trip in the summer of 1964 when the Dercums were trying to run a dude ranch operation there. While the others were out riding, Henry relaxed at the lodge, read, did some sketching and played volleyball. Max even took him on a Jeep tour of the area. Max also remembers when Pete Seibert came by Ski Tip and asked if he could bring in a model of a project he was working on. With favorable response to his new ideas, Pete was able to recruit some of Max and Edna's guests to become investors in the early Vail Ski Area. Among them was Fitzhugh Scott who designed the original Lodge at Vail.

After 30 years of waiting, Max finally breathed life in his own dream in 1970. With the help of Bill Bergman, an Iowa attorney, a group of financiers each putting up $25,000, and Ralston Purina's hefty $1.65 million initial investment, Keystone was transformed from a sawmill and railhead into a ski area. A strict environmental protection plan, designed by the U.S. Forest Service, called for each tree to be hand cut and demanded that trails be extremely narrow — 100 to 200 feet wide, as compared to an average 700-feet-wide ski run. A dry winter in 1973 pushed Keystone to become the first resort to install snowmaking, which also helped cover the remaining stumps.

They had 67,000 skier visits the first year of operation with a network of 16 runs covering 2,300 vertical feet which were serviced by two double chairlifts to the mountain's summit. The upper lodge, then named Keytop (Summit House today), impressed visitors with its eight levels of pitched roofs patterned after the area's prominent mine tipples. An all-day lift ticket or lesson cost skiers $3.50, compared to $55 in peak season of 1999-2000.

"Developing a ski area was slow, hard work in those days," said Max Dercum in a 1971 *Colorado Magazine* interview. "It was the day of the shoestring operation. For a long time the Forest Service was reluctant to expand its skiing surveys. They didn't want to crowd areas close together, fearful that there wouldn't be enough business to support them all."

Still skiing three to four hours each day as they enter their mid-80s, Max and Edna remain optimistic about growing old. When asked how they do it, Edna simply smiles and says, "Enthusiasm is youth. Besides, sliding is certainly easier than walking!"

Max nods in agreement saying, "Skiing has always been a way of life for us."

Bill Bergman

*"My practice my whole life has been putting things together,
be it baseball games or playing hooky from school. I have often led people
into things they probably didn't want to get into."*

—*Bill Bergman on his life as an attorney*

Few people would believe that one of the most popular ski resorts in the United States emerged out of America's Heartland – Iowa. From across the Great Plains, where corn is usually the tallest silhouette against the skyline, came the financial backbone of Keystone Mountain Resort. Bill Bergman, a savvy corporate attorney from Cedar Rapids with the magic gift of turning dreams into thriving businesses, helped transform a rolling, unobtrusive, tree-thatched hunk of Arapaho National Forest into a nationally regarded ski resort, enjoyed by skiers and their families for nearly 30 years.

"My practice my whole life has been putting things together, be it baseball games or playing hooky from school," Bill admits. "I have often led people into things they probably didn't want to get into."

What began as a vision that Max Dercum had fostered for more than 20 years first took shape one snowy Christmas evening in 1968 in a snug cabin near the Snake River. Max had skied every inch of the mountain and surrounding terrain until he had it memorized. With his dream of a ski area close to his heart, he worked diligently on his plans, creating a prospectus, hand-sketching maps and models he hoped would help sell the concept. Until that night, he had been unable to get it off the ground.

A Midwesterner, Bill Bergman had learned to ski on rope tows in Wisconsin in what he describes as "the coldest weather in the entire world." Bill graduated from the University of Iowa where he was a football and basketball player. He met his wife, Jane, a freshman beauty queen, on campus in Iowa City after returning from World War II duty in Italy as a B-24 Lead Navigator in the Air Corps. Jane smiled and teasingly said, "Actually, he was the first one back from the War. That's why I married him." Bill started practicing law in Iowa in 1949.

"I have always loved the thrill of the chase.
Anticipation excites me."

Bill and Jane began their annual skiing visits to Colorado in 1952 and fell in love with Summit County. They stayed at the Ski Tip Lodge or the Alhambra cabin, located one-half mile east of Ski Tip. The Alhambra cabin was owned by Jane's sister and brother-in-law and several of their friends. They originally purchased Alhambra from Edna and Max Dercum, who had lived there while building Ski Tip. Bill and Jane became friends of the Dercums. Subsequently, the Bergmans purchased the Alhambra and it became the official office of Keystone Resort. The Bergmans later donated Alhambra cabin to the Keystone Science School and it was moved to the site of the "Old Town" of Keystone, where it remains.

Keystone Keybase – Photo by Do[...]

You're Invited
to the
Opening Ceremonies
of
The New Keystone Ski Area
11 a.m.
November 21, 1970

Invitation to Keystone opening
ceremonies that ran in *The Denver Post*.

Jane Bergman christening Lift #1 on dedication
day, November 21, 1970, while Bill looks on.

The Bergman family skiing at
Telemark, Wisconsin in 1958.

Keystone in 1970.

Gathered around a fireplace on New Year's Eve of 1968 at the home of Blair Wood, a judge from Waterloo, Iowa, who claimed to be the first ski instructor in the United States and who attracted many other Iowans to the sport, the group began discussing Max's plans. "This was when the enticement began," Bill said. He admits that in the beginning, he really wasn't interested in getting involved, but Max and the others "ganged up" on him until he finally gave in. Bill shook his head remembering how fast it all happened and said, "We saw an entire ski area evolve in a matter of minutes." While Bill had a great deal of experience working with manufacturing and other small business start-ups, this was his first ski area. "I was pretty sure the idea was good, but I told Max to not feel badly if it failed," he recalled.

Bill returned to Iowa from his Colorado ski vacation with a special excitement. With advice from University of Denver economics professor Jim Johnson, they determined what it would take to open a ski area. "We looked to see what Vail had done when they got started and decided we needed to raise $25,000 per individual investor," Bill said. He quickly gathered a group of his clients and spread the plans before them. They responded with enthusiastic nods of yes. With little convincing, he also recruited 15 of the 20 friends he skied with during his "stag years" to become members of Keystone's ambassador corps. All the money was raised within Iowa, with a few exceptions of "knowledgables," such as the Dercums, which simplified the often-complex process of raising funds. The investors were all granted lifetime transferable ski passes as well as one-third acre of land for development. For all his hard work during this four-month planning period, Bill and Jane were granted stock and land options. Today, they live in a home built on one of those plots along the Snake River.

"Our thought was to raise $800,000 to handle the planning for the first year, then initiate a public stock issue," Bergman recalls. "But that didn't prove necessary." Entering stage left was another one of Bill's clients — the Ralston Purina Company of St. Louis.

"You see, I did the law practice for myself.
I did Keystone for Max and Edna. "

"They had the money and were looking for diversification," Bill said. "It simply was one of those deals that happened at just the right time for everybody." Meanwhile, Bill, president of Keystone, trying to build the ski area from his Cedar Rapids law office, hired Vail's general manager, Clay Simon, to run the day-to-day operations. Max saw his dream realized and became the first ski school program director.

In shaping the image of Colorado's newest ski area, Bill described how they wanted to preserve the mining look with a railroad feel, as Vail had adopted the Swiss chalet style. Keystone adopted its name from the old Pennsylvanian miners, but people didn't seem very wild about it at first. They even held a name contest to rename it, but no one submitted anything better. The original logo had three mountains represented: Soda Ridge, Keystone and Independence.

Bill Bergman and the flight
crew he served with in
World War II.
Bill on the far right,
standing, in 1944.

Bill and Jane Bergman on
the bank of the Snake
River near their home.

Today Keystone weaves harmoniously with the original character of the landscape as a result of strict stipulations by the U.S. Forest Service, including installing lifts via helicopter. Keystone opened for business by Thanksgiving 1970 after the Bergmans christened the first lift. "I was bleeding from doing the honors," Jane laughed. "I had glass shards in my face from smashing the champagne bottle. I didn't know you were supposed to wrap it!" In the early days, Jane did all the marketing herself for no salary, by delivering brochures around in her car. She visited ski shops, college campuses and spoke to people, personally trying to generate enthusiasm for a young Keystone. "Jane's a good con artist," Bill said with a smirk.

Bill retired from his law practice on December 22, 1998 and he and Jane made their mountain get-away in Keystone a permanent residence. They ski as often as possible now that they have the mountain in their backyard. One day as they rode up a chair lift together, Jane looked over at Bill and pointing to the acres of tree-lined slopes, asked, "Aren't you just so proud of all this?" While he said yes, that he was, Bill admitted that he was actually prouder of starting his own sizeable law firm.

"You see, I did the law practice for myself. I did Keystone for Edna and Max," he said.

The Bergmans have long enjoyed travel and Bill likes it even more when it is associated with his other passion — golf. For 28 years, with Jane as his caddie, he played in the British Amateurs and with Arnold Palmer and other notable names in the U.S. Senior Opens. He once qualified for the National Amateurs in Pebble Beach where Jack Nicklaus won a week before Jack's first baby was born. Bill's name can be found etched on a plaque at the club in Pebble Beach, listed directly under Jack's.

When he isn't on the greens, Bill can be found trekking somewhere outdoors. He is good friends with Charlie Meyers, editor of the "Outdoors in the West" section of *The Denver Post*. The two of them enjoy duck hunting or fishing when they get the chance. Exemplified in his many life accomplishments and attested by those who have been cast under his persuasive influence, Bill Bergman is a leader who makes things happen.

He just shrugs and says, "I have always loved the thrill of the chase. Anticipation excites me."

Jody Anderson and Phyllis Armstrong

"When we first moved here they were moving buildings all the time.
Almost daily a building would go up the road."

—Jody Anderson on the impact of Lake Dillon to Summit County

Jody Anderson and Phyllis Armstrong learned first hand that geography blended with time equals destiny. What began as a chance encounter as neighbors in sparsely populated Summit County turned into lifelong camaraderie and companionship that has endured the countless tests life doles out.

Jody first met her husband Charles (Charlie) at the Fitzsimmons Army Hospital where she was a nurse. He had been going to school and working at United Airlines. After years of living in Denver, they longed to take their three children and escape the city to start a little business somewhere where life was more carefree. Summit County became the logical choice, with the Dillon Dam being built and Breckenridge ski area just getting its start. "There was so much going on here in Summit County in 1961, it was incredible," said Jody.

Taking a tip from a book club friend, Jody and her husband came skiing in Summit County over Easter weekend to check out a lodge that was for sale. Next thing they knew, they were packing up and moving to Frisco on June 6, 1961. Their new purchase, the Frisco Lodge, had been closed for nearly a year after the previous owners had gone out of business. As a result, Public Service informed the Andersons that they were stuck with the delinquent power bills of the previous owner. "It was astronomical," recalls Jody. "It was certainly an amount of money that we didn't have."

A shortage of housing in the County presented Jody and Charlie with all the business they could handle from the moment the Lodge opened its doors. Many of their customers were workers from Sturgeon Electric, a big contractor on the dam project. They so desperately needed a place to sleep that the Andersons began renting out two shifts of beds at $5 a night. When the guys who worked graveyard would get up to go to work, men on the previous shift would come in and take their beds. "They didn't care. They were just happy to have a place to take a shower and get some rest," said Jody.

Frequently workers came in at night with a case of beer to share as they sat around talking before going out to dinner. One of their favorite places was The Antlers, at the confluence of Blue River and Ten Mile Creek in Old Dillon, followed by a trip to the Dairy King. The A&B Café that used to be across the street from the Frisco Lodge was also a favorite stop. At the time, the Frisco Lodge was the town's largest building. In 1965, Jody and Charlie added on a motel to the backside of the original structure. In an effort to entertain the guests, Jody's kids would sell rides for $.25 or $.50 on a pony named Boo Boo that they kept behind the Lodge. The pony almost always bucked people off, but everyone thought that was pretty funny. "Our kids all had to work because we couldn't afford to hire help. Of course, there wasn't anybody to hire anyway," explained Jody. "It was poor times in the '60s and '70s."

Making progress and beginning to grow, Frisco boasted four restaurants and seven gas stations in the mid-1960s. One, The Blue Spruce, was leased by Phyllis and Dick Armstrong and located near the corner of Summit Boulevard and Main Street. A major oil

The Frisco Lodge in 1948.

The Frisco Lodge in 1962.

company bought land on the corner near the restaurant, forcing them to move it 150 yards east to where the Chamber of Commerce currently resides.

Phyllis remembers the night before they opened the restaurant they varnished the floors and the woodwork, but didn't allow enough time for it to dry before the grand opening. "People would stand up and the chairs they were sitting in would stick to them," she recalled. As the restaurant was getting started, they would often venture down to the water's edge as the reservoir was filling and lay rocks along the shoreline. The next day they would return to see how far the water had risen since the night before.

Like the Armstrongs, the Andersons were quickly establishing a presence in the community. After living in Summit County for only three months, Charlie Anderson entered politics because nobody else really wanted to at that time. Before he knew it, he had been mayor of Frisco for nine years. Many years later, Jody would serve as chairperson of the planning commission and Phyllis spent time on the Frisco sewer board. As a proponent of responsible growth, Charlie met a lot of resistance from many of the local residents who lived in Frisco but commuted to jobs in Climax. They didn't want to see "progress" come to Frisco if it meant paying more taxes in the name of capital improvements. Nevertheless, Charlie encouraged people to come to town and start a business.

Jody recalls a time when a man named Walter Byron, who owned a great deal of land around Frisco and Climax, would take certain people aside and tell them, "I own from the top of that mountain to the top of that mountain to the top of that mountain." At one time, he owned the towns of Kokomo and Robinson before selling the land to Climax. Walter was always very secretive and would only sell land to select individuals, including the Armstrongs.

"We were very adventurous and got into lots and lots of difficult situations on occasion. It's amazing we all survived all those many years."

While Phyllis and her husband were busy building a cabin across the river from the Frisco Lodge in 1963, their three children were off making friends with their new neighbors, the Andersons. From that moment on, a tight bond formed between the two families and they became known as the "Anderstrongs," since rarely would one be seen without the other. Unlike many children today who rely on television and electronic games for entertainment, nature served as the playground for the Anderstrong group.

"When we first moved here, the children were wonderfully free," recalled Jody. "They were free to roam the hills."

In 1962 there wasn't a lot of development on the north side of Ten Mile Creek, and Fourth Avenue ended where a bridge had not yet been built. The kids especially enjoyed playing around the creek, where they had secret swimming holes and would be outdoors from morning until night. "On New Year's Eve, our kids would all ski up North Ten Mile or up Peak One and spend the night," said Phyllis. "They called it their initiation."

Phyllis Armstrong at home with her piano.

Jody Anderson with sign from the days when the Frisco Lodge was known simply as "The Hotel" in the late 1930s and early 1940s.

When any of the parents needed to round up the throng of children, they would walk along the creek until they came upon a bunch of dogs and there they would find them. "We wandered all over and the kids wandered all over. They were very self-sufficient," said Phyllis. She said it was not unusual for the children to take off on their own and go camping when they were just 10 and 12 years old. The only house rule was that the they had to write a note telling both sets of parents in which direction they were going.

The children all learned to ski as a natural part of life in the mountains. "Back in those days we only paid $.50 for the kids to ski and that included lessons," said Jody, remembering that the children were usually involved in some kind of mischief at Arapahoe Basin when they went to take their lessons. Jody started a Nordic ski shop in 1967 with the help of Jim Balfonz, the coach of the high school ski team. Established in conjunction with the Frisco Lodge, the ski shop was formed to ensure that the local kids, including Jody's daughter Cheryl and Marie Zdechlik's daughter Kris, who were on the women's U.S. Ski Team, had access to good ski equipment.

By this time, the Anderson and Armstrong parents had also become close friends and enjoyed many of the same activities together, including fishing, hiking and backcountry jeeping. "We were very adventurous and we got into lots and lots of difficult situations," admitted Jody. "It's amazing we all survived all those many years." One time when they had taken their Jeeps off-road, they got stuck on Georgia Pass. "We had the two dogs, the six kids, one orange and one Hershey bar," laughed Phyllis. When they could afford it, they would sometimes go on excursions to places like Glenwood Springs. Otherwise, they had fun playing games, including Bongo Boarding. They also went to movies on Sunday nights that were shown in an old army Quonset hut which is now the Colorado Log and Antler Company in Breckenridge. In the winter, it would be so cold that they would take sleeping bags or quilts to keep warm.

Jody and Phyllis have remained trusted friends for more than 36 years. Since arriving in Summit County, they each have been afraid to wear multiple hats when it came to vocation. Jody served as a family planning nurse practitioner from 1974 until 1982. She also founded the Frisco Gold Rush, Colorado's first Nordic citizens race, which began as a fundraiser for children's skiing. As a result, there is now a trail at the Frisco Nordic Center named "Jody's Nugget."

Phyllis has always been a music-lover. She was the vocal music teacher for Summit County schools for 25 years, teaching K-12 since 1965. In 1999, one of her former students was touring with Mickey Rooney in the stage production of *Wizard of Oz*. The auditorium at the Summit Middle School is named after her — The Phyllis Armstrong Auditorium. One year, she taught a bunch of school kids to sing the Norwegian National Anthem for Olav Pedersen's Ski for Light event that was held in conjunction with the Frisco Gold Rush. Over the years, Phyllis has also played the piano in more than 287 weddings.

"We didn't get rich very fast, in fact, we didn't get rich at all, but we sure had fun," said Jody.

Phyllis nodded, adding, "It just wasn't in the plan, I guess. Looking back, I think our kids had the most fun when we were the poorest."

❄

Bob Craig

"I moved to the ranch to become a
'high altitude Henry David Thoreau.'"

—Bob Craig on his brief life as a rancher

Defining Bob Craig is like trying to capture the wind. Yet his contributions to Summit County, and on an even grander scale, to the world, are noticeably apparent in his achievements as skier, climber, philosopher, rancher, teacher, speaker, reader, author, policy shaper and leader. Along the way, he has made the acquaintance of many notable individuals such as Hunter S. Thompson, Jon Krakauer, Madeleine Albright and Hazel O'Leary. Bob even became fishing companions with Supreme Court Justice Byron White.

Since he was young, Bob has been inspired to climb simply because he loved the fun of it. He has honed his leadership skills by taking each challenging step, pushing human limitations and touching the extreme boundaries of man's world. Growing up in Seattle, Washington, Bob became interested in both skiing and mountaineering at a time when they hadn't yet become popular. Following the European mountaineering tradition in an organization called "The Mountaineers," he made a number of first ascents in the Cascades and surrounding peaks. He began ski racing in 1939 when he was in high school and started traveling around the state and to Sun Valley, Idaho, a year or two later. At that time, most everyone was expected to ski "four-way," which meant they competed in downhill, slalom, cross-country as well as jumping in order to earn enough points to make the team. Ski technology evolved dramatically while he was competing. Some styles of bindings literally glued you to the skis and didn't release like safety bindings. It was while wearing skis with inflexible cable bindings that he severely injured his leg in 1941, breaking it in 14 places during a downhill race called the "Silver Skis" on Mount Rainier. The ski patrolman actually fainted when he came to help Bob and saw the bone sticking out of his pant leg. When another accident in 1946 left him with a broken back, he quit racing.

During World War II, Bob followed his father's footsteps and joined the Navy even though many of his friends went into the 10th Mountain Division. He believes his interest in philosophy was originally ignited by his War experiences. Bob was a deck officer and acting chaplain aboard the first ship that docked at Nagasaki after the atomic bomb was dropped. He also walked into the center of Hiroshima about five months after The Bomb had been dropped there. Philosophy continues to permeate nearly every aspect of his life, whether on mountain tops or during international gatherings with diplomats and business people.

When he returned from the War, Bob revived his love for climbing by conquering first ascents on Devil's Thumb and Kate's Needle in Alaska. A year later, in 1947, he returned to Alaska to climb Mount McKinley and explore the Arctic Circle. He also operated a guide service on Mount Rainier from 1949 to 1951. Bob then accepted a teaching fellowship at Columbia University where he completed his Ph.D., with the exception of his dissertation, in philosophy. Then during the Korean War, Bob was offered a position as a civilian consultant in the Army's Mountain and Cold Weather Training Command, teaching mountaineering and cold weather survival at Camp Hale and Fort Carson. In 1953, Bob was presented a career opportunity by Walter Paepcke, chief executive officer of the Container Corporation of America and one of the founders of

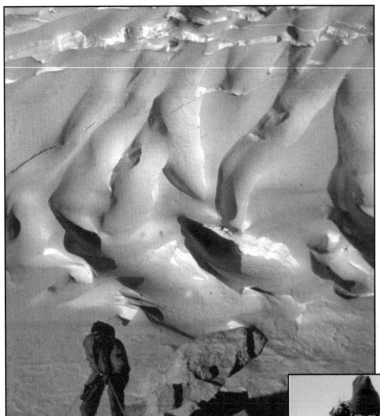

Bob Craig being helped off the Goodwin-Austin Glacier near the base of K2 by Hunza porters in 1953.

Bob Craig on belay on Mount Everest in 1983. Photo by Galen Rowell.

Bob Craig in Antarctica in 1988.

modern Aspen. If Bob could survive his trek up K2, the world's second highest mountain that had only been twice attempted by Americans, then he could have a job with the Aspen Institute, a world-renowned think-tank. Storms left one climber dead and prevented the group from reaching the summit, but Walter gave Bob, with his severely frost-bitten feet, a job as his assistant. Later, Bob became the executive director of the Aspen Institute for Humanistic Studies. While at the Institute, Bob helped shape its direction and was involved in inviting speakers. Of the nine Supreme Court justices, seven spoke at the Institute during Bob's tenure. Among the high profile decision-makers and upper-level business leaders, Dean Acheson and Gerald Ford also spoke.

"The idea was to get corporations to think about larger problems in society in a humanistic way, beyond just the bottom line of profit," Bob explained.

After 12 years at the Institute, Bob decided to move on and become, as he puts it, "a high-altitude Henry David Thoreau." He and his former wife bought a 1,200-acre ranch on Woody Creek outside of Aspen in 1963 and ran a cow and calf operation. When his Walden experiment failed due to his lack of interest in the cowboy lifestyle, Bob started an industrial design company in Denver.

Bob seemed to feel a void when he stopped climbing and soon, the call of the mountains drew him back to new, vertical challenges. He co-led the first American expedition to the Pamirs, a range in Russia virtually unclimbed by outsiders, or Russians, for that matter. The expedition turned tragic, as the entire seven-member Soviet women's team was killed in addition to eight other climbers, including Bob's tent-mate, Gary Ullin. Bob amazingly survived the avalanche that struck the tent he and Gary were sharing. A second avalanche struck and buried him again before the rescue team could arrive. Bob recalls that being "unquestionably the most despairing and hopeless moment of my life... near death and resurrection twice within 30 minutes."

The devastation of the accident deeply affected Bob, so he moved to his present home in Keystone and spent some time writing. The result was an account of the expedition, *Storm and Sorrow in the High Pamirs*. Despite the risks, climbing was still in Bob's soul and he led another successful expedition, this time an American trip without oxygen up the West Ridge of Mt. Everest in 1983.

After spending time regrouping, Bob decided it was time to tackle yet another new project. Years earlier in San Francisco, Bob had met Bob Maynard, a former assistant director of the National Park Service and founder of the Yosemite Institute in Yosemite National Park, which is a field education and experiential education program. Maynard asked him if he had "another Aspen" in him because Maynard had the vision of creating The Keystone Center. That's when The Keystone Center and Science School were born.

R.W. Craig
Former Naval Person
Mountaineer and Alpinist
Philosopher
Humanitarian
Environmentalist
Thane of Montezuma

Sketch by
Hank Parker

Bob Craig in one of his favorite pastimes, fly-fishing.

Bob had the Aspen Institute in mind but tried not to duplicate it as he developed the new nonprofit organization in 1974. He thought the timing was ideal for addressing issues that were coming out of the National Environmental Policy Act and the mountain environment would serve as a place of "remove" where people could discuss and resolve issues. During the first couple of years, The Center was mostly concerned with the issues of high-level radioactive waste. The Keystone Science School was designed to teach children basic understanding about the environment, focusing heavily on the sciences. Now,64 more than 3,000 children attend the school's various weeklong residential field science programs which include lessons on geology or botany in hope of making them more informed adults. In addition to the camp programs, the Science School also presents the Wilderness Adventure Program. Another program known as "Cops and Kids" was hugely successful in helping children who may have been heading toward juvenile delinquency.

Currently, Bob is working on the National Commission for Nuclear Threat. Its goal is to develop a national policy on the threat of loose "nukes" and unregulated materials in the former Soviet Union, as well as in North Korea, Iran and Iraq. Bob and staff work to facilitate the meetings of the minds. He said he feels very fortunate to have been able to accomplish what they have through The Keystone Center. The "Scientist to Scientist Colloquium" is one program of which he is particularly proud. Over the years, more than a dozen Nobel laureates have come to speak to younger scientists from many diverse fields to encourage cross-fertilization between the various disciplines of science.

After a lifetime of exotic travels, adventures and political gatherings, Bob continues to be drawn back to Summit County because it is a relatively low-key place with a good quality of life. And with the exception of his service in the War, he has never left the mountains for any significant amount of time. He hopes to spend as much free time as possible skiing and fishing, because with all the business traveling he continues to do, Bob acknowledges that he "has a hard time on city streets in wing tips."

Bob still enjoys skiing fast and "scrambling around on rock" when he has the chance. However, he has had his left ankle fused (in the angle of a Lange ski boot, he added) after an injury, and a more recent ski accident prevents him from doing some of the more technical climbing he loves.

Pride for Summit County still rings strong in his voice when he talks of his beloved mountain community. "I hope that the lives of the people in this book will set a standard whereby newcomers to the County will recognize what it took to live here," he said. "I think that there's a lot of very special spirit here."

❄

Gene and Ina Gillis

*"We couldn't even come to see our new house because there was this great big,
fat beaver sitting right in the middle of the road. He wouldn't let us pass by.
That's how primitive it was."*

—*Ina on first moving to their home in Keystone*

Like many others attracted to Summit County, Gene and Ina Gillis came in 1971 for the great mountains and dependable snow. As avid skiers, they wanted to live in a place where the powder was sure to fall every year. They discovered a young Keystone.

"We couldn't even come to see our new house because there was this great big, fat beaver sitting right in the middle of the road. He wouldn't let us by. That's how primitive it was," recalled Ina, describing their move to Keystone.

"We raced in everything.
Clouds, rain, snow.
It really made no difference."

Gene met and married Ina while he was employed in Canada by Staedli Lifts, a Swiss ski lift manufacturer. She was his German interpreter. A common interest that drew them together was their passion for skiing. Ina grew up in Geneva, Switzerland and had been introduced to the sport by the time she was 4. She moved to England and then to the United States with her family, but went to Canada for college. Gene, too, had a European influence while he was growing up. He started skiing in 1927 and trained with a number of Norwegians and Swedes in Bend, Oregon. It was there that Gene learned how to stop, snowplow and jump. Jumping was a very popular activity then.

His father had actually handcrafted Gene's first pair of skis. Gene said that at the time, nothing differentiated alpine from cross-country skis. They were all built as cross-country models with leather straps to offer greater mobility. They sometimes used door springs that hooked into the skis to hold the heel down. The Super Diagonal came later. These bindings were made of rubber, which had a spring that held the boot better than leather had. Gene said, "Basically the skis would break before the bindings released!"

When Gene started racing, there were only the downhill and slalom events. He said the main difference in skis for each event was merely length. In 1947, Gene skied the U.S. National Championships on a brand new pair of skis that Gary Cooper had discarded. "We raced in everything," said Gene, reflecting back on his early ski racing days. "Clouds, rain, snow. It really made no difference."

Gene Gillis at Mount Bachelor, Oregon, in 1947.

Gene and Ina Gillis in Arizona in the late 1960s.

If needed, racers would sometimes add a burr to the skis' edges to help control the skis on ice. Gene admits that he loves figuring out how to best prep skis for the different conditions racers encounter. Gene was on the U.S. Olympic Team in 1948, "before television" he likes to say, the year the Olympics were held in St. Moritz, Switzerland. Three weeks before competition he was hospitalized for a diabetic condition and unable to participate. Later that same year he ended up placing in the top 12, twice in competitions in Austria.

Arriving in Summit County during its infancy, Gene was seeking a new professional challenge. He first worked for Larry Jump preparing a small ski resort outside of Denver called Arapahoe East, which never opened for operation. He then met Max and Edna Dercum and the Keystone management team who hired him to develop Keystone Mountain, much as he had done at various resorts around the country, including Stratton Mountain in Vermont and the Arizona Snowbowl in Flagstaff.

"All you can do when you ski is turn left, turn right and go straight. The way I see it, you can do all that right here in Summit County."

Max had already done a lot of work on the mountain, but he invited Gene to walk around North Peak and Jones Gulch to make recommendations on what to do next. At one point, he even thought it might be feasible to connect Keystone with Arapahoe Basin.

Having previously been employed by Sno•engineering, one of the original companies to embrace snowmaking, Gene's first course of action was to go to the Water Board to check snowfall in the area. He informed them that snowmaking would be crucial to the fiscal health of the ski resort based on its snowfall figures. Once he received the go-ahead, Gene installed snowmaking at Keystone. Snowmaking was actually first developed accidentally by a farmer in Massachusetts who feared an early frost would damage the fruit in his orchard. He rigged up a mister to spray his trees as protection. After being distracted by a lengthy phone call, the farmer walked back outside to check on his orchard, only to discover a mound of snow beneath his apple trees.

Beyond snowmaking, Gene shared other insights with Max from his previous ski resort experiences. He showed everyone how to groom the snow properly in the winter months, as well as how to prep the hillsides in the summer to maximize the conditions. He advocated seeding wildflowers and grass and removing all the tree stumps that were hazards to skiers. Gene also was at the forefront of an innovative concept called "snow farming," which involved pushing excess snow into the woods on the sides of the trails for use later on.

Gene Gillis at Stratton Mountain in 1962.

Gene Gillis and friends at Mount Bachelor, Oregon, in 1947.

In addition to being an aggressive competitor when he was younger, Gene had coached a great deal. He decided that Keystone could benefit from a bit of competitive instruction. In 1980, Gene got together with Bob Craig, Bob French and Peter Witter to form the Summit County Race Team. Gene primarily worked with young Olympic hopefuls. He wanted to develop a system whereby potential racers could get together with various coaches and race in different places throughout the year. The racers would work with coaches from each of the Summit County areas and train on different terrain. To his students, he strongly emphasized the importance of good grades and often repeated a common refrain, "There are four things that you need to do: you have to eat; you have to sleep; you have to do your school work well; and you have to ski. In that order." U.S. Ski Team member Jason Rosener is one of the most recent success stories coming out of the Summit Race Team.

Gene taught Ina how to instruct, first in Canada and then in Flagstaff. When they moved to Colorado, Ina was accepted by Max and Rolf Dercum to be an instructor with the Keystone Ski School. In 1985 when the Mahres opened one of their Training Centers at Keystone, she was one of the instructors introduced to their system of skills development. Soon after, she happened to give a beginner lesson to a young lady who told her that she was signed up for the very first Mahre Camp starting the following day. Since she was the only beginner, Ina was asked to coach her and has been with the Mahre Camps ever since, specializing in beginners and low intermediates. The rest of the winter she is still part of the Keystone Ski School.

During her first summer at Keystone, Ina was asked to revegetate an area near the river that had been disturbed during the building of the Keystone Lodge. Ever since, she has spent her summers taking care of the landscaping throughout Keystone Resort.

Even after 28 years of living in Keystone, Gene and Ina haven't felt compelled to stray too far to pursue the sport they love. Gene said, "All you can do when you ski is turn left, turn right and go straight. The way I see it, you can do all that here in Summit County."

Ina nodded her head in agreement and jokingly replied, "I have no desire to go anywhere else. This is our home. Gene and I are going to raise pigs and chickens right here. Aren't we?"

❄

Gert (Culbreath) Young

*"The thread through my entire life has been
getting on a horse and heading for the backcountry."*

—*Gert Young on her love of horseback riding*

She was a girl on a horse. For Gertrude (Culbreath) Young, the ride has been exhilarating, the journey fetching, haunting and draining. Along the way she has discovered many new frontiers in both landscape as well as within herself. "The thread through my entire life has been getting on a horse and heading for the backcountry," said Gert. "I have always loved to just go riding high into the hills where I can look around and think." As her refuge and solace, Gert has long enjoyed riding up and down the many hidden trails of the Lower Blue. One of her favorite haunts is above timberline on Blue Ridge where her father, Cully Culbreath, used to run sheep and where she can take in a panoramic view of the Gore Range, the Williams Fork, Lake Dillon, the Ten Mile Range and even on to Wyoming. That sense of adventure and intense desire to wander still stirs in the depths of Gert's soul.

Born the first of three children to Elizabeth Engle and Henry Grady (Cully) Culbreath, Gertrude was named after her grandmother, Gertrude Briggle Engle, who was married to Swiss immigrant, George Engle. George and his brother Peter owned and operated the Engle Brothers Bank in Breckenridge where the present Exchange Building is located. George died in 1926 making Gertrude Engle the honorary president until they voluntarily liquidated the bank during the Depression in 1936. She continued to reside in the family living quarters upstairs in the bank building where Anna Strand, Edna Dercum's mother, later came to help care for Gertrude after her health failed. Gert appreciates having known her "Grammy" and treasures the antiques she remembers gracing the old parlor, dining room and other quarters of the Engle house and which Gert now includes in her own home.

When Cully and Elizabeth were first married, they bought a ranch "down the Blue," midway between Dillon and Kremmling. Gert and her brothers, Grady and George, were born in Kremmling. Growing up very involved in the many ranch chores, they also made time for fun. Though their grandmother, a strict Methodist, never really approved of dancing and such, Elizabeth was extremely social. Dances and gatherings held at the old Lakeside or Slate Creek Halls involved the whole family – baby baskets and all. Elizabeth was a charter member of the Blue Valley Home Demonstration Club where she and neighbor ladies organized family pot-lucks, picnics, holiday parties and other events that provided many happy and helpful experiences for all ages. Less than a mile from the Culbreath ranch house sits a huge rock in a grove of "quakies" (Aspen trees) where Gert remembers her mother planning picnics and birthday parties, while hoping the cows wouldn't decide to camp there the night before as the area wasn't fenced in.

Construction on the Green Mountain Dam project began during the late 1930s, creating the need for food and housing for the construction workers. The demand for milk kept Cully busy buying more milk cows and eventually a barn where he started Cully's Big Rock Ranch Dairy. Grady and George helped milk cows twice a day. Unless she could escape on the back of one of her horses, Gert washed bottles or helped with chores in the house. Belonging to 4-H Club cooking groups in Grand and Summit Counties helped Gert learn to enjoy cooking and baking. "Mother used to get a little upset," remembered Gert. "I would put the cake in the oven then go for a horseback ride and forget the cake."

Gert Young at age 3.

Gert Young and her
mother circa 1947.

Gert Young at Arapahoe Basin in the mid-1940s,
before the chairlift.

Gert's parents built five cabins to house construction workers' families, later renting them out to fishermen and hunters. Though there were other children living on the ranch part of the time, Gert remembers it being a bit lonesome. "Horses were my buddies," Gert proclaimed, fondly remembering Duke, her first, then on to Rowdy, Peggy, Topsy and Smokey. When Gert was a baby, her dad had a hard time getting her on a horse. But it wasn't long before he had a hard time getting her off.

At times the Culbreaths owned 25 to 30 horses that they used on teams in the hay field to feed the cattle during the winter. Gert became very adept at harnessing her own rake team to take hay out to feed the range cattle. "I would do just about anything to get out of housework," she said. "I always preferred being out on my horse." Sometimes she rode the work horses, which she compared to "sitting on a dining room table." Gert preferred to ride bareback, considering saddles a nuisance. Eventual back surgery serves as a reminder of being thrown off numerous times over the years.

School has changed a great deal for ranch children since the Culbreaths were enrolled. The old Lakeside school where Gert started first grade was made up of a cloak room and a single classroom that housed eight grades. Located on the floor of the valley now covered by the Green Mountain Reservoir, it had no electricity or indoor plumbing. Gert remembers everyone trying to crowd around the lone heating stove during the winter, with the windows completely covered with frost on cold days. Realizing there were educational "gaps" in the system, Elizabeth used her teaching degree in high school English and history to tutor her children at home a great deal throughout their school years, much to their dismay as they would have preferred being outside.

---

*"You have to make the land work for you.
Our family has always been very enterprising. "*

Elizabeth also insisted the children be "exposed" to piano lessons, Gert recalls, so once a week after chores, the family piled into the old 1938 Chevrolet to take lessons from Kenneth Caldwell in Frisco. "After years of trying to get us to practice and struggling through piano recitals probably were enough to convince her that no musical talents lay uncovered. She had 'done her duty,'" Gert laughingly said. She credits her mother for working on her and her brothers manners, appearance, religious teachings and other things she considered important to help them not be "country bumpkins."

When Gert was ready to enter high school, her parents borrowed money to buy the Valaer dairy ranch to be closer to the only available school bus transportation in Summit County. Today the Valaer is known as the Neal Smith ranch and Willow Brook now sits where the old milk cow pasture once was located. The bus would pick up students in Dillon and drive them to Breckenridge High School, the same school from which her mother had graduated in 1921. However, Breckenridge changed from the bustling, prosperous town Elizabeth grew up in to a near ghost town when mining all but vanished from the community. Gert remembers Breckenridge as very depressing during those years, with little to do and jobs hard to find. There were only seven other classmates in her graduating class of 1950.

Gert Young and elk antlers from a hunting trip in the 1960s.

Gert Young's Senior Picture, 1950.
Credits in annual included:
President of Student Council, Editor-in-chief of Annual,
Pep Club, Dramatics Club, Glee Club one-half year.
Favorite Sport: Riding or Skiing
Favorite Subject: History

Having played semi-pro baseball during his younger days, Cully loved sports and passed that enthusiasm on to his children. Gert remembers her parents hauling loads of kids to basketball games wherever Breckenridge High School played when she was a cheerleader and later when her brothers were on the team. With no school bus providing transportation, the team and pep club traveled by car to games in Walden, Hot Sulfur Springs, Red Cliffe, Fairplay, Climax, Minturn and a now defunct mining town of Gilman.

During this time, Cully sold the milk cows and took over the Meadow Gold Dairy agency supplying most of Summit County during construction of the Roberts Tunnel, Dillon Dam, I-70 and Eisenhower Tunnels, as well as the ski areas. Selling the Valaer ranch around 1967, the Culbreaths moved to Breckenridge where Cully continued his dairy delivery route. Gert remembers escaping with her brothers to the ranch near Green Mountain Dam every chance they got, to work, ride or whatever as they found Breckenridge extremely boring.

During the late 1940s, Edna and Max Dercum introduced many Summit County children to skiing. Gert recalls that an old army truck was used to haul skiers from Highway 6 up into Arapahoe Basin to use a rope tow before the chair lifts, t-bars and Poma lifts were built. As adults, Gert and Edna maintained their friendship and enjoyed reminiscing. Over the years, Gert had enjoyed occasionally working at Dercum's Ski Tip Lodge waiting tables, washing dishes or whatever Edna needed done. "After work in the evenings, everyone would sit around the wonderful old fireplace Max built, laughing, singing and talking," Gert recalled.

Having had business training in Denver, including working for Public Service downtown at their old G&E building, Gert went to work at the Climax Molybdenum Company in 1955, replacing Jackie Gorsuch Evanger, another good skiing friend, as technical librarian. While living at Climax, she shared an apartment with Susy Randall, a teacher from Michigan who later became George Culbreath's wife. Climax mining company provided a lighted ski hill for night skiing with a ski hut at the base where someone would play accordion or other musical instruments, providing what Gert describes as hours of "homespun fun."

In 1957, Bob Young and Gert, who with Bob's parents purchased the Maryland Creek Ranch near Dillon, were married. The biggest part of the ranch operation was pasturing yearling cattle and raising hay to sell. Among Gert's ranch projects were training horses, helping with cattle and in the hay field, cooking for the crew, keeping the deep freezes stocked with home-made bread and meals to fix in a hurry, keeping books and whatever else fell her way. To help make ends meet, Gert got her outfitters and guides licenses and started Gore Range Trail Rides. She used mostly horses she'd broken to pack groups into the Gore Range, dropping them off to camp, picking them up later or allowing them to back-pack out at their leisure. She and Bob also raised Shetland ponies that turned out to be great "babysitters" for their three children, Kandice, Kerrill, Robert, Jr. and many of their friends. At times there would be as many as six children riding the ponies, always bareback, and Gert would take her children and friends on pack trips each summer.

Fall hunting season was reserved as Bob and Gert's vacation, alone or with friends and relatives. "Though we loved the adventure

Gert Young riding her horse, Chipmunk.

of hunting, we used the meat to stock our freezers," Gert said, adding that over the years she probably created 365 ways to fix elk and venison. "This is my country," declared Gert. "It is in this territory that I have done a lot of riding and hunting. I could pull an elk out of country you could barely ride a horse – and probably shouldn't have in some cases."

After Bob's death in 1975, Gert continued to run pasture cattle on the Maryland Creek ranch, which they had sold but were leasing back. Finding good help to take care of 600 or so head of cattle as well as the irrigating and haying became impossible, so she ended the lease in about 1982. Gert had leased part of the Lazy YO Acres, which she still owned, to a gravel company, being very careful to make sure the pits maintained a natural appearance and resembled ponds for fishing.

Beginning in 197 and until just recently, Gert rented out her ranch house short-term during ski season, and the yard for weddings and events in the summer until terminating the business in 1998. The setting became so popular for young couples that she reluctantly turned down more than 20 potential wedding couples. "You have to make the land work for you," said Gert. "Our family has always been very enterprising in making ends meet and attempting to deal with supply and demand, much of it on borrowed money that had to be paid back on time."

Remarrying in 1983, Gert and husband, Don Stuwe, are able to spend part of the winter in Arizona. Gert's son Rob and wife Lynette have a ranch management consultant company that includes Gert's property among its clients. Of course one of the top priorities is that Gert's horses be shod and ready to ride. Don teases her, saying that riding with Gert means mostly being lost. She smiles and shrugs, "I've often been accused of never following a trail, but I still prefer to jungle crash."

If ever friends drop by to pay Gert a visit, only to find the door open but the house empty, they would be wise to look toward the hills. Somewhere deep in the thickly wooden mountain sides overlooking the Valley of the Blue, will be a girl on a horse testing her boundaries.

※

Bud and Martha Enyeart

"We grew up in a small community. Raised our kids in a small community.
Today, Bud and I continue to enjoy life here in Summit County.
We want to be here as long as we can."

—*Martha Enyeart on family life in Summit County*

To Carl "Bud" and Martha (Loomis) Enyeart, home is not just a place to hang your hat, but a community of family and friends and a sense of belonging. They grew up in a time when being a member of a community meant more than just eating and sleeping there. It meant getting involved, looking out for your neighbors and taking stock in civic pride. "We grew up in a small community. Raised our kids in a small community. Today, Bud and I continue to enjoy life here in Summit County," Martha said. "We want to be here as long as we can."

Civic involvement was nothing new to Bud and Martha. It all began with Martha's great grandfather, C.C. Warren, who graciously donated the land for the Dillon cemetery, and her grandmother, who became the first telephone operator in Dillon. In 1940, Bud's father was elected Summit County Sheriff, followed by Martha's father in 1946. Her father also worked various jobs around Summit County, including painting, hanging wallpaper, hard rock mining on the Dredge and finally serving as Sheriff, where he died in office.

Born on a ranch on the Lower Blue in 1924, 17 miles north of Silverthorne, Bud Enyeart was the middle son of nine children. He attended Slate Creek's two-room school and helped with chores on his father's dairy such as hauling hay to feed the cattle and milking twice a day. His family moved back and forth from the Lower Blue to Breckenridge beginning in 1929. He later went to high school in Boulder because the only upper level school in Summit County was located in Breckenridge, which was an impossible commute for ranch children living in such distant rural areas. In Boulder he traded work with his uncle for room and board.

After serving in the military, Bud returned to his birthplace of Summit County. To him, it seemed like the natural thing to do. "This was always home," he said. "This was where I was born, raised and where I knew people."

Bud followed in the tradition of active town involvement. For 35 years, he volunteered for the local fire department. He was a County Commissioner for 24 years beginning in 1950, when he received $90 per month payment, and was appointed Breckenridge Town Manager in 1972. During his tenure, they paved half of the town's roads beyond Main Street.

An only child, Martha moved to Old Dillon at age five and later attended Breckenridge High. When she was in the second grade in Kokomo, Martha recalls a snowstorm so severe that the railroad — their main source of supplies, food and transportation — had to shut down for 90 days. Avalanche danger was at a high due to 40- and 50-feet drifts. It took nearly 200 men to shovel snow slides from the tracks. This was during a time when her father was mining and their family was living in Kokomo. Her dad resorted to snowshoeing to Climax to pick up food on a toboggan.

Four years Bud's junior, Martha did not meet Bud until he returned from the service. Bud's older sister was getting married when he and one of his brothers overheard a band practicing. They walked up to the house and invited Martha and her band to play for

The crew at the Country Boy Mine at
Christmas in 1942. Martha Enyeart's father,
Ray Loomis, is far right in the back row.

Underground at the
Wellington Mine in
1949. Bud Enyeart is
third from the left in the
back row.

the Shiveree, a surprise party for the newly wed couple, and a dance at the Swan's Nest. She played an accordion in a high school band called "The Kids." They attended dances in those days at the old Breckenridge High School gymnasium, Slate Creek Hall and Dillon Town Hall. Shortly following that night at the Swan's Nest, Martha and Bud began dating and married not long after.

"We would travel to wherever they had a dance," Martha said. "There was no television, so we had to do something for entertainment." She also participated in a women's bowling league for some competition. Bud enjoyed fly-fishing all over the County. On weekends, she, Bud and their three children enjoyed picnicking and spending time with the many relatives that lived nearby.

Martha described the many fun festivals in Breckenridge where the entire town gathered to celebrate. Breckenridge held an annual picnic at Carter Park on August 8 followed by a dance to observe "No Man's Land." It started in 1936 when the Breckenridge Women's Club announced that a 90-mile-long by 45-mile-wide area including Breckenridge had never been included in the various acquisitions of the United States. Another celebration started in the 1960s by four Norwegian boys was "Ullr Fest," paying homage to the Norse god of winter. Much like today, there was a parade with an honorary king and queen and a dance at the Bergenhof, the base lodge on Peak 8. During one parade, Bud pulled members of the Broncos football team on the fire department's hook and ladder float. In 1948, Gilda Gray, a flapper called the "Shimmy Queen" in Hollywood, made a guest appearance at a No Man's Land celebration and stayed with the mayor. "She was a real shot in the arm," recalled Martha.

Another draw that served as a social thread to Summit County during the middle part of the century was the more than a half-dozen active lodges and fraternal organizations in Breckenridge. During Martha's 50-year membership in the Rebekah's, she enjoyed the teachings, the friendship and the fellowship with other members. Bud continues his active membership in the Masons with 60 others involved in the Breckenridge chapter. However, he says the average Mason in Colorado today is 72 years old and dwindling participation makes recruitment of younger members increasingly challenging. One of their daughters was a Rainbow Girl, an organization for the daughters of The Masonic Order and The Eastern Star group, and their son also participated as a Mason. Other active groups included the Grand Army of the Republic, the Woodmen of the World, the Elks, Daughters of the American Revolution, Sisters of Mustard Seed and Eastern Star. It wasn't uncommon to find a lot of crossover in membership, as many people belonged to more than one group. "The lodges were a big thing in those days," explained Martha. "It was very important to belong to a group and get together. This is one of the things we did."

Between 1947 and the development wave of the '60s ski boom, only two new houses were built in Breckenridge, one of them by Bud and Martha. During that first year and a half of marriage, Bud built the mill in Montezuma and worked in St. John's mine in search of lead and silver, throwing out what zinc they came across since it was considered worthless. His main form of transportation was to cross-country ski back and forth to the mine. Once Breckenridge opened, he and Martha bought a season pass for $20 and began to ski recreationally whenever they had a chance. He also worked a silver mine near Red Mountain called Fredonia and served as a mine supervisor in Climax for 16 years, beginning in 1956.

Bud and Martha Enyeart walking on Boreas Pass near Baker's Tank. Bud was the first to suggest that the railroad ties on Boreas Pass be removed so that it could be opened to auto traffic.

Bud also built a second mill to the east of Copper Mountain and worked that for a while. He was involved in all aspects of mining, from mine developing to production and milling the ore. "I made a living at it, but I never struck it rich," Bud said. To him, the most interesting aspect was leasing a mine for a royalty. That means if anything was discovered in the mine, the lessee could keep it with a percentage of the profits going back to the owner. There is a gamble of course, because if nothing is found, it was considered a loss. The demise of mining came to the small operations, such as the Wellington in Breckenridge, in the 1970s. As the final decade of the 20th century bades farewell, there are no longer any operating mines in Summit or Lake counties. The Black Cloud mine closing winter of 1999 in Leadville ended an era that defined the town and surrounding area for 140 years.

As a resident who witnessed a number of economic changes in Summit County, Bud believes the Eisenhower Tunnel and the emergence of the ski resorts had the most significant impact on the area. Martha remembers living through what she called "the scare" as one of the Dillon families who began waiting from the moment the earliest rumor circulated that their town might be flooded by the dam. Denver had plans for the reservoir back as far as the 1930s. "People didn't know what was going to happen or how it might affect them," Martha recalled. "Residents got little value out of their houses and as a result, they weren't left with enough money to turn around and buy new homes. Many had to scramble." When the new town of Dillon emerged, there were only about a half-dozen houses in the beginning. They even had to move the cemetery, where many of Martha's relatives were buried, to make way for the reservoir. Her mother also moved her house to Breckenridge where she lived the rest of her life.

At one point Breckenridge had even been "redlined," meaning it was in the financial danger zone. "We did everything we could to attract business," Bud explained. "There just wasn't much going on. Once we started planning, zoning and putting in sanitation codes, the interest in Breckenridge grew."

Bud said that if it weren't for the ski area, the town would probably still be economically depressed. Skiing really brought the town to life. The Rounds and Porter Lumber Company of Kansas saw some potential in the County in the late 1950s and began buying up land that was on delinquent tax lists. They originally intended to use the land for a saw mill, but ended up building a ski area instead. "When the Rounds family bought more property," Bud said. "that's when things started to happen."

"I would have liked to see a slaughter house built – anything to encourage people to come to Summit County. Anything that would bring payroll to the community," he said, talking about the decline of mining and the advent of World War II that left Breckenridge a shell of the bustling town it once was during the silver boom. Until the Bank of Breckenridge came on the scene, there wasn't even a financial institution in town. Residents had to travel all the way to Kremmling or Leadville to do their banking.

"There was a time when we considered moving," Bud admitted. "That was back when things were so depressed, we couldn't afford to move anyway. People talk about the 'good old days,' but in my opinion, these are the good old days. Today we have people, business and things going on. Now that things have picked up and are finally getting interesting, I'd like to stick around to see what is going to happen."

※

"Ski patrol has really been most of my life."

—Chris Beger on ski patrolling

Looking back on his 52 years of active involvement with the patrol, Chris Beger admitted, "Ski patrol has really been most of my life." Founded in 1937 by Minot Dole, the National Ski Patrol System (NSPS) has played an integral role in the ski resort business. Chris smiles when he remembers that he first joined the patrol as a display of male machismo, often performing stunts that reflected his fearlessness. "We would start up in Imperial Bowl, ski down, hit a ramp and jump all the way over the ski patrol shack and land down on the opposite side," recalled Chris on skiing the Breckenridge Ski Area. "That was when I was young and stupid."

It didn't take Chris long to reach a point when he recognized that the reason for being a member of the patrol was for the satisfaction of aiding people in distress. He gained a great deal of fulfillment from determining what was wrong and discovering what needed to be done to help someone. "When you're in uniform, you never pass a fallen skier," he said, taking seriously his responsibility to uphold skier safety. "The goal is to always leave the injured person in better condition than when you found him."

Today, at age 76, Chris continues to wear his uniform proudly as the most senior member of Keystone Resort's ski patrol. He says they affectionately treat him like a grandfather now. "I'm like the football player who just won't quit," he laughs. This depth of experience has given him a keen eye for what it takes to succeed in the patrol and now each spring when the new candidates arrive to try out, Chris can usually tell who will make it and who won't. "I think it's an attitude," he explained. "Those people who see the patrol only as a free lift ticket won't cut it."

Growing up in Denver, Chris visited Summit County for the first time in 1935 at age 12 when he accompanied his father on a business excursion to a mine at the defunct town of Tiger for Kenyan Ironworks. He remembers crawling inside a "classifier," which is a wooden apparatus that separated different sized ore, and helping to scrape out the gold dust residue that would stick to the inside of the machine. In those days, gold was worth $35 an ounce. Chris worked for a number of years as an apprentice for the machine shop before the start of World War II.

In 1940, at only 17 years old, Chris joined the mule pack in the 10th Mountain Division at Camp Carson. After a few short months, he grew weary of mules and transferred to the Military Police Guard escorting German prisoners back to Europe from Africa in the heat of the War. He then served in an engineering company for about six years in the South Pacific. In 1946, Chris was discharged from the military and hospitalized in Fort Logan in Denver for a year as the result of a shrapnel wound. He also returned from his tour of duty with a case of malaria.

Back in Colorado with the War over, injuries healed and his life to plan, Chris decided to channel his love for skiing into a volunteer position with the ski patrol in 1947. "All 50 volunteers," Chris explains, "were responsible for their own uniforms and first aid supplies for the first 15 years. It was also their responsibility to adhere to the National Ski Patrol and emergency medical technician (EMT) training as recognized nationally."

Chris Beger "on duty" in
the Philippines in 1945.

Chris Beger in the surroundings he likes best.

Chris Beger on the trail
at Keystone that is
named after him.

In 1957, Chris became a member of the Berthoud Pass Ski Patrol and was appointed first aid chairman of the Rocky Mountain Division at Berthoud Pass ski area. For fun, Chris remembers skiing 16 miles from the top of Berthoud Pass all the way to Winter Park. He became a full member of the NSPS in 1960. Transferred to Breckenridge in 1961, Chris served as the head of the NSPS Candidate Program and was patrol leader. While in Breckenridge, he and his wife, Thelma, rented a small ski chalet behind the El Perdido Mexican restaurant on French Street. In the early years as the ski area was just getting its start, there were no buildings along what is now Ski Hill Road or any built all the way to the present day Peak 8 parking lot. He does however, fondly remember some of the popular eating establishments of the day. "We loved going to the Hoosier Inn," said Chris. "The woman there used to make the best hamburgers."

Chris served on the patrol at Breckenridge until 1970 when he went to Keystone to help organize the ski patrol there. Keystone's original National Ski Patrol group consisted of people from different ski areas who started meeting at the Ramada Inn in Denver. Once the Keystone patrol got organized, Jim Morton came from Winter Park to run it. Most of the volunteer NSPS patrolmen that first year at Keystone came from a small ski area called Meadow Mountain near Vail, which Vail had purchased and shut down when Vail opened. There were about 50 volunteer patrolmen and only six full-time paid patrolmen. At the time, volunteers earned one lift ticket for each day they worked. The year Chris arrived, lift tickets at Keystone were only $9. They had been $7 at Breckenridge when it first opened and increased about $2 per year.

Keystone gained the reputation of being a rather mild mountain in the first years, because only the front side had been developed and there wasn't as much difficult terrain – especially for a daredevil like Chris. As the ski area expanded, the terrain became more diverse and challenging. However, Chris remembers skiing the steeps of Jones Gulch for avalanche and winter survival training.

During his years of patrolling, Chris rarely missed a weekend at either Breckenridge or Keystone. Even during the two years he lived in Albuquerque, he would drive up to Keystone on Friday night, patrol Saturday and Sunday, and return to Albuquerque on Sunday night. In three years, he put more than 60,000 miles on his car and never missed a weekend. Today, every member of Chris and Thelma's extended family – nine grand children and eight great-grandchildren – has benefited from his many years of service on the patrol with a season ski pass.

In 1980, Chris and Thelma built the house they currently live in, and moved from Denver to Summit County to live permanently in 1987. When he is not on the mountain, Chris and Thelma enjoy as many activities as they can manage. Although the season is short, they have always especially adored summer. Over the years they have spent a lot of time sailing on Lake Dillon and today, they go power boating on Lake Powell. Other favorite activities include cycling, rafting and now, motorcycling. Chris has ridden his motorcycle to Flagstaff, Tucson and Juarez. Mostly, however, he has always enjoyed being in Summit County because of the people who live there. "We have a lot of very close connections with people who live here," he said. "I imagine we will probably end up staying there for the rest of our lives."

✳

Summit Pioneers

93

Grady and Gail Culbreath

"We sure missed it. While we were down here on the ranch
worrying about 'cow units,' Max and Edna (Dercum) were at Keystone
worrying about 'people units' and look how that turned out."

—Grady Culbreath on ranching in Summit County

First there was the land – the dirt, pastures and vast openness of the Lower Blue, acres upon acres just south of Heeney. Then there were the Culbreaths, the salt of the earth and one of the bedrock families of Summit County. The two blended well together, a partnership of quiet respect and such subtle boundaries, exemplifying a symbiotic relationship of hard work and bountiful resources.

Grady Culbreath's grandfather came to Grand County at the turn of the century from Switzerland where he had been a dairy farmer. He owned the Engle Brother's Exchange Bank in Breckenridge. Grady's mother and father grew up in Breckenridge. In 1929, she and Grady's father purchased the ranch in the Lower Blue and raised their three children, Grady, Gertrude and George, in the same house Grady and his wife, Gail, live today.

When Grady was a child, the 63 counties in Colorado were numbered according to population. Denver, for instance, was given number 1 and Summit County was so sparsely populated that it was assigned number 61. As an established family in the County, Grady's parents acquired the first license plate issued – 61-1. Later, the "61's" were changed to "ZL."

When Grady and his brother and sister were young, there were at least five different schoolhouses scattered along the countryside between Dillon and Kremmling to accommodate all the ranch children. Grady attended first grade in a one-room school house that today would be located at the bottom of Green Mountain Reservoir. Green Mountain was part of the Colorado Big Thompson Project that began in 1940 and was filled in 1946 or 1947 to help the growers in Grand Junction. While the dam was being built, there were approximately 30 to 40 of the workers' children enrolled in the school in Heeney. Grady's parents rented out five cabins on their property to house the dam workers and also sold them milk and eggs.

"Ranching is all I ever wanted to do."

In those days, it wasn't unusual for children who lived down the Blue to temporarily live with other families in order to be closer to school and avoid the long commutes. After first grade, Grady attended Lakeside in Heeney, then Dillon, where he had his first classes with his future wife, Gail (Byers). They then attended high school in Breckenridge, graduated in 1953 and were married three years later.

Grady laughed, recalling how he met Gail and said, "A hunter once asked me, 'Where did you find her?' I just replied,

Gail Culbreath at work in the corral.

Grady Culbreath junior class photo.
Credits include:
Student Council, Glee Club,
Basketball Forward,
Favorite Sport: Basketball
Favorite Subject: Physical Education

Gail Byers junior class photo.
Credits include:
Class President, Pep Club,
Dramatics Club, Glee Club
Favorite Sport: Riding
Favorite Subject: Mathematics

Grady Culbreath with Gail in the background.

'Oh, in the third grade.'"

Gail, also a Summit County native, was born in Breckenridge. Her grandparents owned a ranch just beyond the gravel pit near Maryland Creek. Her parents lived in the old town of Tiger when she was born, where a lot of cattle were summered and tended by a "pool rider." Grady thought that there must have been about 1,000 cows in the ranchers' "pool" between Dillon and Kremmling. At one point, the Byers owned the Tenderfoot Ranch, which is now covered by the Lake. It was a 2,000-acre parcel, including Corinthian Hills, that the City of Denver purchased for around $200 per acre to build Lake Dillon. Her father built one of the two Water Board houses that still stand. Gail's family moved to the town of Pando by Camp Hale where they ran a dairy. They delivered milk to Red Cliff and Leadville. Ranchers would put cream in five gallon cans out by their mailboxes to be picked up and sold by dairies like the Byers'. It was a large part of life on the Blue River in Summit County. Gail remembers how the tops would pop off the milk bottles when winter temperatures dropped below freezing. Grady's father also delivered milk around Breckenridge for Meadow Gold for many years.

While hard work often consumed much of a rancher's life, there were also many opportunities to gather with friends and neighbors and have fun. "The Fourth of July was bigger than Christmas," explained Grady. On the Fourth, there were rodeos with all the festivities and celebrations. Gail's father furnished bucking stock for the Dillon Rodeo.

"Everybody competed," said Grady. "The girls would barrel race and we'd ride bucking horses, cows and calves." His brother George became a good saddle bronc and bareback rider and went on to win the collegiate competition in the region in 1960. Today, Grady's grandson Clay enjoys riding steers and won three belt buckles competing last summer.

In the early part of the century, there were two types of people in Summit County – ranchers and miners. At one point or another, Grady found himself wearing both hats. There was a time when many of the ranchers purchased Mexican longhorn cattle with the vision that this would be the new trend of the future. Then the meat market crashed and a lot of the ranchers went with it. According to Grady, the crash "broke some pretty strong, old ranch families on the Blue." His grandfather offered support where he could by loaning many people money during the hard times and was never repaid.

Life as a miner wasn't much easier. When Grady's mother lived in Breckenridge, she often talked about the 400 or more miners who came into town from the Wellington and other mines after a shift for some fun. However, when the gold market took a dive during The Great Depression, this all changed. Many mines either shut down or reduced staff accordingly as demand dropped. Grady and George both worked in the Wellington Mine during Christmas and spring breaks while they were in school to earn extra money. Once mining died out, Breckenridge turned into little more than a ghost town.

In 1960, Grady and George had the opportunity to purchase the ranch from their father. That same year, Grady began a dual career as an outfitter, which he continued to do for the next 15 to 20 years. Gail kept busy raising five children and often cooking for the hunters that were allowed to lease the ranch for hunting. "Ranching is all I ever wanted to do," said

Grady and Gail
Culbreath moving cattle
at Otter Creek Ranch.

Grady.

Today, they summer 500 to 600 cattle, as well as some they pasture for other ranchers. They expect to winter 150 to 200 of their own cows on the ranch near Kremmling. They also pasture 150 dude horses and plan to complete a horse center soon for people to stable their "hobby" horses. Additional revenue continues to come from hunters. In the past, as needed, the Culbreaths have sold parcels of land to help fund college for their children.

"Fortunately, we learned pretty early on that you don't just sell the whole thing (the ranch), but maybe you peel off what you have to and stay in for the rest of the ride," Grady explained.

"Before the ski areas were built, the concept of people buying second homes in the mountains was a foreign one," said Grady. The boom of the ski business directly impacted the appreciation of their land and helped the Culbreaths stay in business over the years. Nearly 15 years ago, after witnessing the growth of the sleepy Lower Blue they once knew, the Culbreaths put some of their 1,200 acres into a conservation easement to prevent future development.

"When you see your land's original value per acre now being valued about the same per foot in a single lifetime, then you know you've seen a lot of changes," said Grady in disbelief at the continuous rise in land values throughout the county. "Of course, these values really mean nothing to us. We don't plan to sell, so they really don't matter. Quite frankly, the only reason we are still able to live here is because we *were* here."

The Otter Creek Ranch.

Olav Pedersen

*"We didn't talk about 'alpine' and 'cross-country' skiing then.
We had skis and we used those skis for going up on the
mountain and for jumping. That was skiing."*

—Olav Pedersen on growing up skiing in Norway

Olav Pedersen has helped blind men see. While miracle worker isn't on the list of his many talents, he has shed light on skiing — a sport long thought to be off limits to the blind and physically handicapped. His vision has enabled many people from all walks of life to see beyond their bodies' limitations and share his enthusiasm, passion and joy of skiing.

Born in 1917 in Voss, Norway, Olav was introduced to a world at war, with food rationing and other wartime hardships, and entered manhood at the start of World War II. He served in the resistance movement during the German occupation from 1940 to 1945, then resumed a career with the Norwegian State Railroad. In 1955, after a lifetime of skiing and ski racing, Olav was given the distinguished honor of serving as the organizing chairman of the 1955 Norwegian Skiing Championships held in his hometown of Voss. Voss was also the birthplace of the famed Norwegian-American and Notre Dame football coach Knut Rockne; Olav initiated the erection of a monument paying tribute to this great sports hero. While Olav has had quite an impressive list of challenges and experiences, he claimed that his greatest life accomplishment was Ski for Light, a program he created in the United States in 1975. The program was designed for visually impaired or physically handicapped people to enjoy cross-country skiing or ski touring.

"You just have to get out there and do a good job.
That means that you do it for them. Don't discourage new skiers by showing off,
because that has nothing to do with teaching."

The idea materialized one early morning in 1952 as Olav was walking to the train station and he ran into a group of blind musicians who had just arrived on the night train from Oslo to Bergen. He introduced himself and offered them a ride to their hotel, which they graciously accepted. They then asked him to emcee their performance that evening. As complete strangers to one another, the idea seemed crazy, but nevertheless, Olav agreed to do it.

"I've never had more fun in my entire life," recalled Olav. "The audience was fantastic."

He was so energized by the experience, that he rushed home and wrote an article about the group's leader, Erling Stordahl, who was Norway's most popular musician and he sent it to a couple of newspapers and magazines. Olav then asked Erling to be the star performer at the 1955 Norwegian Skiing Championships. At that time, the musician confided in Olav that he had this vision of teaching the blind to ski. He said that he had tried skiing blindfolded, and he was able to maneuver around the mountain by snapping his fingers and listening for the echoes. That moment never escaped Olav's heart. He thought that if such a program could work in Norway, then it would surely be a success in the States as well. Nearly 20 years later, it continues to shine.

Olav Pedersen on the left
at age 15 with his brothers.

Olav Pedersen holding
the St. Olav's medal
presented to him by
the King of Norway
for his efforts in bringing
Ski For Light
to the United States.

Olav out for an early morning ski at the Breckenridge Nordic Center.

Olav learned to ski when he was around 3 years old. He wore a pair of skis that didn't even have bindings other than a small strap to hold them on. He practiced on a little hill located on his father's land until he was 9 or 10 years old when he began competing in jumping events. Cross-country skiing was never his first love until he was older and started witnessing long-distance runners racing on skis. "We didn't talk about 'alpine' and 'cross-country' skiing then. We had skis and we used those skis for going up on the mountain and for jumping. That was skiing," Olav explained. For the past 12 years, Olav has competed in the Senior Games in Breckenridge and has taken home many medals. In 1988, he won the National NASTAR Championship for his 70-years-and-older class in cross-country skiing in Steamboat. Already featured in the Colorado Ski Hall of Fame, Olav has also been nominated for the National Ski Hall of Fame.

In 1964, Olav brought his skiing experience to Breckenridge and began a second career as an alpine ski instructor for 16 years. When he first arrived in Summit County, there were only six or seven other ski school instructors compared to the more than 400 that exist today. He first lived in an old mining cabin, which he recalls was pretty drafty and cold.

"One thing about being in the mountains, you always feel like you're surrounded by friends."

As an instructor, Olav was always in high demand for private lessons. He often had more requests to teach than he was able to accommodate. His secret, he said, was simple, "You just have to get out there and do a good job. That means that you do it for them. Don't discourage new skiers by showing off, because that has nothing to do with teaching." In 1980, the same year he stopped giving lessons as a ski school instructor, Olav coached the U.S. Nordic Olympic Team participating in the Olympics for the Disabled in Geilo, Norway. He also helped prepare the representatives for the U.S. Ski for Light to participate in the Norwegian Ridderrennet competition in 1983.

Yet it was Ski for Light, which happens to share his own birthday, February 17, that was Olav's true pride and joy. Celebrating 25 years in 2000, Ski for Light was modeled after the Knight's Race (Ridderrennet) in Norway with international participation. Held annually, Ski for Light matches one sighted guide/instructor for every participant on a one-on-one basis to help teach skiing to as many disabled people as possible, with the idea that they may continue to enjoy the sport after returning to their home communities. Olav boasts that some of his guides have been with the program for more than 20 years. Ski for Light works because it provides balance – nourishment for physical, social and emotional needs. Most importantly it begins with the "If I can do this..." insight into one's own greater potential that is experienced by both skier and guide and is the start of significant lifestyle changes. It has been a highly successful way to bring together handicapped and non-handicapped people from throughout the United States, Canada, Norway and other countries. Even though the first event, held in Breckenridge, only had 60 participants, the program was off to an enthusiastic beginning.

Olav Pedersen skiing at the
NASTAR Finals at Snowmass, Colorado.

Olav at the Breckenridge
Nordic Center.

"The support we had was just incredible. The whole community wanted to get involved. Even Fort Carson got involved," recalled Olav. Former Governor Dick Lamm embraced Ski for Light and volunteered to be one of the guides. The event has since been held in other venues such as Minneapolis and Woodstock, Vermont. The goal was to move it around in order to create more awareness for the program. Today, they recruit more than 7,000 participants from five to six countries to be a part of Ski for Light International. In 1976, Olav was honored by Norway's King Olav with "St. Olav's Medal," as a symbol of good relations between Norway and the United States. He also received an invitation to the White House, met former President Gerald Ford who was given a one million kroner gift from the government of Norway for establishing a health sport center much like the one Erling Stordahl had opened in Norway.

The town has without question felt the impact of Olav's contributions over the years since he established a home and many dear friends in Breckenridge in 1964. He met his second wife, Suzanne, while caroling during the Christmas of 1964. Continuing to enjoy outdoor excursions and acting in the Backstage Theater, neither of them show any signs of slowing down. Their zest for life is an inspiration to anyone who is near.

"I don't think it was ever my idea to live here the rest of my life, but that's what it will probably be," said Olav, smiling about the three decades spent in Breckenridge.

"One thing about being in the mountains," he added. "You always feel like you're surrounded by friends."

❄

Marie Zdechlik

"It's difficult to teach children how to ski, as they want to head straight down and go fast. They learn best by watching and mimicking."

—*Marie Zdechlik on teaching children how to ski*

Marie Zdechlik possesses the firm resolve of a determined soul. The mischievous glint in her eyes sends a strong message that no chance, destiny or fate can hinder or control her spirit. Marie possesses a bedrock of strength and energy instilled from her childhood and enforced through the rugged mountain lifestyle she adopted more than 50 years ago.

Marie feels grateful for the independence her father and mother taught her on the farm where she grew up in Minnesota. Neither of her parents had more than a seventh-grade education, but they had a lot of "hard-knocks" learning. She clearly remembers her father sitting her down one day and saying, "Now that I've raised you and paid your way for 18 years, let's see what you can do." Those who know Marie would say she has more than proven herself capable of doing just about anything she sets her mind to. She has never been one to wait around for someone else to do things for her. If ever there was something she didn't know how to do, she just dove in and tried it anyway.

"You learn to do all these things because you have to do them," Marie said. "No one can teach you anything if you don't want to learn. Learning is a privilege."

During World War II, Marie joined the U.S. Cadet Nurse Corps, which was designed to increase the number of nurses supporting the war effort by paying the enlistee's entire tuition. She graduated in 1946 and moved to Colorado, where she worked at the University of Colorado Hospital with the Red Cross during the polio epidemic, caring for children with the disease. The gym was turned into a ward with 160 children, ages 18 months to 16 years. As one of six nurses on a shift, Marie explained, "We gave baths, physical therapy, hot packs, read stories, sang songs and anything else that might help make their stay less painful and lonesome." During those years in Colorado, Marie also helped her sister with her new baby as well as attempted skiing for the first time. "I think I fell 45 times in Winter Park, but I knew I would some day master skiing," she said, admitting that she has always thrived on new challenges.

Marie then moved to Climax in 1947, where about 500 workers lived with their families. She went to work in the daytime for $1 per hour and $1.08 for the graveyard shift in the Climax infirmary. The hospital was fully equipped and staffed for emergency care as well as inpatient and outpatient care, including occasionally delivering babies when bad road conditions prevented people from making the drive to Leadville. She joined a bowling league called The Panhandlers with a group of other nurses. In the summer, fast-pitch softball became the free-time activity of choice and Climax sponsored a women's team on which Marie played. They traveled to Leadville, Basalt, Glenwood Springs and to the state tournament in Denver. Also at that time, Mount Massive Golf Course was in the early stages of development, so Marie and a group of her friends decided to play a round. "Tufts of grass made up the fairways, the roughs consisted of sagebrush and the greens were sand. From that day on, I became a golf-aholic," said Marie.

Skiing was just gaining recognition in Colorado in the late '40s when a t-bar was installed at Climax. The terrain was still quite

Christmas stockings hanging above
the Zdechlik family fireplace.

Marie and Bob
Zdechlik in 1965.

L-R: Matt, Lisa, Bob, Kris, David, John and Joel
Zdechlik on the hill near their house
in Frisco in the 1960's.

rugged by modern standards. A lift ticket was $10 a year and Climax was open Wednesday and Saturday nights as well as weekend days. Marie said, "If you could ski Climax, you could ski anywhere." Having mastered the sport, she joined the ski patrol. One of the largest concerns for the patrol was the boys from the 10th Mountain Division at nearby Camp Hale. Many of the soldiers were from places like Alabama and Georgia with no opportunities until now to ski, so when they crashed, they crashed hard. Referring to the older equipment technology, Marie said, "They weren't safety bindings. You could fall on your face and you would never come out of those bindings."

On New Year's Eve of 1953, she married Bob Zdechlik, a math and science teacher at the Climax School. He had been stationed at Lowry Field and like Marie, had become an avid skier. They lived in a one-room apartment during that first year of marriage and Marie continued to work up until the day she delivered their first child. After becoming a mother, Marie ran the ski patrol at Climax. Many people that skied during the years Marie worked at Climax remember her coming over the loud speaker and yodeling to the crowd.

Climax began experiencing geographically altering changes in the late '50s as residents were asked to move their houses in order to make room for more mining. Marie explained that the residents moved to the east side of Fremont Pass and by 1962, all homes were moved to Leadville. As a wedding gift, a long-time engineering friend gave Bob and Marie three 25 feet x 140 feet lots in Frisco and they purchased six more. Armed with books on construction, plumbing and electrical wiring, they began building a home in 1954, moved in 1958, added on in 1960 and filled the last nail hole in 1964. "With only 87 people living in Frisco in 1954," explained Marie, "it was challenging to find help with the construction, which is why so many do-it-yourself houses began to spring up."

"You don't have to win, just do your best. If you start something, finish it."

Marie handled the challenge well. She did all her own rock work on their fireplace even though she had no previous experience. Marie and Bob also dug their own well, which was only 42 feet deep, using a frame and old miner's technology, and installed a pressure pump. Water was continually a scarce commodity, even through the '60s. It would typically freeze, forcing people to resort to other methods, such as melting snow to wash their hair or bleeding the fire hydrants and using buckets to fill their bathtubs. They also had to keep their septic tanks open to keep them operating or else they too would freeze solid as well. Bob accepted the daunting task of becoming Frisco's water commissioner during these challenging times. The eternal optimist, Marie said, "What are you going to do? Cry about it? No, you just had to keep laughing." With four of her soon-to-be six children keeping her busy, Marie said she had no time to complain.

Motherhood began taking more of her time and focus, yet Marie made certain she instilled many fundamental life philosophies in her children as they were growing up, just as her parents had instilled in her. She would tell them, "You don't have to win, just do your best. If you start something, finish it."

Marie enjoying one of her favorite pastimes, golf.

Marie Zdechlik out
walking with her grandchildren.

The schools began including skiing as part of the curriculum, but the children still couldn't get into a formal class unless they could snowplow and turn; ski schools were also in their infant stages at that time and did not have enough instructors to handle the large number of students. Marie and Jody Anderson, another longtime Frisco resident, set out and cut down a bunch of trees to make a little ski hill for the children to learn on. When the children were good enough, they would go to Arapahoe Basin and practice skiing around poles to further enhance their ability. Marie began shuttling carloads of 13 or more young children to Arapahoe Basin every Saturday to learn more about the sport.

Mothers of skiing children volunteered to help with beginners on the instruction hill. Those who didn't ski helped to put on skis and mittens, wiped noses and told them how great they were, Marie recalled, "It's difficult to teach children how to ski, as they want to head straight down and go fast. They learn best by watching and mimicking."

Many children in the area took an interest in Nordic skiing when Steve Reischl and Jim Balfonz came to Summit County and introduced ski touring. Parents also got together and built ski jumps at the base of Royal Mountain for them to practice jumping, which had also gained in popularity. By this time, the youngest of Marie's children, who was just five years old, was also ski jumping. The kids would foot-pack the ramps for take-off and landing, and Marie would help set the track on the in-run of the ski jump. "I didn't want to jump, but when some little kid says, 'Mrs. Zdechlik, would you set tracks for us?' you don't want to say, 'No, I'm too scared to jump.' You just get into a tuck and then stand up. That's all you do," she said matter of factly.

All of the Zdechlik children were skiers. The girls skied alpine at a very young age and branched out into cross-country and jumping. They competed for Summit Schools and in Rocky Mountain Division races both nationally and internationally. Each reached their own level of competition, taking them as far as college. In the spring of 1971, Bob took a vacation and the entire family, with children ranging in age from 5 to 17 skied every day. Marie recalled, "We packed a picnic lunch the night before and went skiing at Arapahoe Basin, Keystone, Breckenridge, Copper Mountain and Vail. It was a week full of fun-filled days with many laughs and something the family talked about for many years."

Marie became the local favorite of the neighborhood children, always playing an active role in their fun and discipline. She, with the mothers' and children's help, built a baseball field for the local children in a nearby meadow where Mountain Side Condominiums are now. Many a home run rolled into Jug Creek.

Today, Marie maintains and lives in the same home she and Bob built years ago and even uses her own table saw for those occasional "projects" that arise. Bob always shared her zest for life until his death in 1991. They both have cross-country trails named after them at the Frisco Nordic Center – R.J.'s Vista and MarieZ – forever preserving their spirit of carefree joy in Summit County.

❄

Alf Tieze

"I had to pay two dollars to see myself crash."

—*Alf Tieze on the first time he saw himself in a Warren Miller ski film*

Alf Tieze has always known "the hills" as a place of refuge. Although today he escapes to them to be alone with his thoughts, and to explore vacant mines in the high country of Summit County, he remembers all too vividly when mountains symbolized life or death.

The sleepy mountain village in Austria where Alf grew up, which is now part of the Czech Republic, instantly changed the day Hitler's troops marched in during World War II. "You suddenly had to greet your friends differently," Alf explained. "If you said the wrong word, you were already marked by the Nazis." During the Nazi occupation, his father and adopted mother were both killed. His grandparents and sister were shipped to a prisoner of war camp while Alf, just a boy of 12, was off chasing chickens and hunting for food in a nearby village that had been evacuated with the threat of advancing Russian troops who had broken through German lines. In the meantime, Alf and a boyhood friend rode their bicycles back to the village and discovered they had been left behind. Eventually the Germans caught them as the Russians continued to advance.

They were then sent to a relocation camp where Alf was reunited with his sister and grandparents. The ache of hunger affected everyone at the camp, so Alf and his friend would sneak out to steal food for the others. For a second time, they returned from their hunt to discover an empty camp. Russian soldiers captured the two boys while they were sneaking back in and separated them, sending Alf to work in an agricultural collective run by the Russians. Alf recalls major depression setting in. "I had the feeling that the War was my fault because of all the bad things that continued to happen to me."

Eventually Alf escaped to the West after being chased by police dogs and shot at by Russian border guards. It took him two weeks to get out of the country while aiding an old man on the journey. "I had big clumpy wooden shoes with old inner tubes nailed on the bottoms so they wouldn't make so much noise when we walked," recalled Alf. "Nobody in the camps had regular shoes. All we got were wooden shoes."

For two nights, Alf and the old man hid silently by the Bavarian border and observed the guards in order to time their escape. Finally making a run for it, they were forced to cross a small river while the Russian guards were yelling and shooting at them. As Alf breathlessly crawled up the bank on the other side, he found himself in Bavaria staring directly into the barrel of a machine gun. Much to his relief, it belonged to an American soldier.

Alf then spent time in several refugee camps. He remembers standing in line for hours waiting for meager daily rations. One day, in a camp outside Nuremberg, Germany, Alf was called into the office of the camp administrator. Instructed to go into town to a social services office, Alf was assigned to become a brewery apprentice. With introductory papers in hand, the brew master invited him in and offered him a beer. Having not eaten a decent meal in more than a year and a half, Alf gladly accepted the beer along with some cheese and bread. A small bunk in the brewery became his new home and Alf began his apprenticeship.

Postcard of the original lodge at
Arapahoe Basin, circa 1963.

The Arapahoe Basin Lodge
in flames in December 1964.

Alf Tieze skiing in the 1960s.

When he was summoned to the social services center a second time, they decided to send him to the experimental "Boy's Town" Germany, outside of Munich, Germany. While there, Alf discovered that his grandparents were in East Germany. A letter from his grandmother informed him that his sister was in an orphanage. Not long after, a letter mailed to his grandmother was returned stamped "Addressee Deceased." Trying to hold on to the few family connections that remained, Alf continued to write his sister and in 1961, succeeded in having her smuggled out of East Germany. A year later, Alf traveled to see her for the first time in 17 years. She had since married and had two children. "I became a brother, a brother-in-law and an uncle all in one visit," remarked Alf. His niece eventually came to visit Summit County and attended for one year at Summit High School.

Hearing the call of the mountains once again – this time as a happier beckoning – Alf made his way to Colorado and worked in Denver. He fondly remembers doing a lot of mountain climbing and exploring old mines, like the ones on Independence Mountain in Keystone, through the inspiration of the book *Stampede to Timberline*. While living in Denver, he would drive to Arapahoe Basin whenever possible and ski. At this time, a lift ticket cost $1.50 per day. He remembers when the board of directors proposed raising the daily price to $2.25, many people were appalled and said that there was no way that anyone would pay that much to go skiing. They quickly discovered the number of skier visits weren't affected in the slightest as the price increased.

The skiing bug first infected Alf when his grandfather taught him at age 6 or 7 on a hill near his home in the Austrian village where he grew up. Alf explained how a cross bar was placed between the tips of wooden skis while they were being stored to keep the tips from straightening out. A block was also used between the skis under the bindings to maintain the camber. A leather strap served as a binding. "You used galoshes or whatever boots you owned to go skiing in those days," said Alf. "You certainly couldn't turn the skis – they were like downsized 2x4s and they were extremely heavy. Of course everybody else's gear was the same, so nobody knew the difference."

For 10 years from 1961 to 1971, Alf managed ski shops and taught ski school at Arapahoe Basin. Alf recalls that, "everyone wanted to be an instructor in order to get the parka and the patch, the pin and all the gadgets to impress the ladies." Perhaps it was an effective strategy as Alf met his wife, Sunni Dercum, while interviewing to become an instructor himself. Arapahoe Basin featured the Willy Schaeffler/Gart Brothers/*Rocky Mountain News* ski school each weekend, which drew the largest number of skiers of any ski school in the United States. There may have been as many as 2,300 people taking lessons on any given weekend. Alf and others also would visit places like East High School in Denver and give demonstrations on short skis developed by Howard Head (founder of Head skis) that could be used for training on indoor carpeting. In the summer, he helped build lifts and do other on-mountain maintenance. At the time, holes for new lift towers were dug by hand.

Alf vividly remembers awakening the night of December 5, 1964, when someone, banging on his apartment door (above Arapahoe Basin's rental shop), screamed that the Swiss chalet-styled base lodge was on fire. Alf quickly went to work making sure than everyone was evacuated. It was extremely cold, so many of the car batteries were dead and the cars had to be pushed away from the building. The next morning, with the debris still smoking, the usual throngs of avid skiers showed up, eager to hit the slopes. They

Alf Tieze with the East Wall
of Arapahoe Basin
in the background, 1999.

L-R: Gene Zenger, Alf Tieze and photographer John Russell
at a skibob race in Europe in 1974

sold hot dogs out of the rental shop. "We'd rent ski boots and the ketchup and mustard would be dripping into those old lace-ups. But we got by. It was amazing," recalled Alf.

In 1968, Alf worked with a group to start the first amputee ski program in Colorado, which lasted for three seasons at Arapahoe Basin. Alf personally developed one of the first retractable "outriggers" for amputee skiing. "That was really the most rewarding teaching I ever did," Alf recalled. "It was absolutely unbelievable. Here, the patients had a chance to find out that, 'Hey, there's something I can do!' " He noticed that the amputee skiers would often learn faster than skiers without physical handicaps. Within two weeks, they would be skiing intermediate runs and soon after, participating in races and winning awards. Alf distinctly remembers when an amputee, who had just left the hospital, came out to ski. Upon reaching the top of the Poma lift with no prior skiing experience, he started down the mountain unable to stop and crashed into a giant snowdrift at the bottom of the run. When people ran over to see if he was all right, he looked up and exclaimed, "Man I was lucky. If I'd have had a leg, I would have broken the darn thing!"

Also in 1968, Alf discovered skibobbing, an activity that is similar to bicycling on snow. By sheer coincidence, the Austrian skibob demo team was headed over Loveland Pass when they stopped to skibob at Arapahoe Basin and wandered into the rental shop where Alf was working. They let him try it and he instantly took a liking to the sport. He eventually won the National Skibob Championship two years in a row and competed in many races in Europe. One year after winning the National Championships, Warren Miller called and asked if he could film Alf skibobbing at Arapahoe Basin. For the shoot, the cameraman told him to slide off a cornice on the West Wall and make a sharp turn. Alf had never attempted this stunt before, nor had he ever ridden the new "test" model skibob until that day. The snow was icy and as Alf shot down and turned off the cornice as instructed, he remembers thinking, " 'Oh my God! There's nothing!' It was like jumping off a 10-story building." As soon as he flew off the cornice, the front of the skibob turned and pointed at Alf. He let go of the handlebars, pushed the skibob away from himself when he realized he wouldn't be able to land and crashed very hard in front of the cameraman, who nonchalantly said, "Retake." He did redo the stunt, the second time with success. "They never showed that one. They only showed the explosion," said Alf. "When they showed the movie in Keystone, I had to pay $2 to see myself crash."

During his final year at Arapahoe Basin, Alf became the general manager. When he finally left, Alf went on to become an instructor of Ski Area Technology at Colorado Mountain College in Leadville from 1971 to 1976. During one downhill training session in the winter of 1971, a skier who was not supposed to be on the racecourse ran into him. Due to the injuries sustained from the crash, Alf did not eat solid food for nearly two years. The following year, he underwent knee surgery. The accident allowed him time to pursue his other passion, architectural design. Over the years, Alf has designed and built numerous houses in Summit County.

Alf just has to gaze out one of his large picture windows at his home in Montezuma when asked what has compelled him to stay in Summit County. The mountains, the great snow and the abundant recreation are just three reasons. "My favorite pastime has always been crawling around the woods way up there in the hills someplace."

❄

Summit Pioneers

Melvin and Frances Long

" 'A pleasure ride,' I said, 'What the devil is that?'
When I get on a horse, I'm going to work.
I'm not taking any pleasure ride."

— Melvin Long on riding horses

A thousand acres. It is a piece of land of almost mythic proportions. Yet despite its grandeur, Melvin and Frances (Marshall) Long could probably describe every inch of their once 1,256-acre ranch as they might describe one of their children. While they have reduced their homestead to 856 acres, it is no less impressive. Melvin laughs at many people today who live on two acres and call the land "agriculture." He said, "They couldn't grow enough off two acres to live for 15 minutes."

For the past 50 years they have lived in the same house in the Lower Blue where both Frances and her father were born. The room that now serves as a kitchen was once the full extent of the original house. Frances' grandfather had originally ventured to Summit County to become a stagecoach driver in the 1880s. During those early years, he ran a livery stable in Dillon and drove a stagecoach route from Buena Vista to Leadville. Later, when he began raising a family, he started ranching.

"I guess I thought it would be a pretty good life to live.
If you're in it for the money,
forget it."

Melvin grew up in Nebraska, but moved to Kremmling at the age of 14 or 15. Frances had been working at a bank in Kremmling when they met and they continued to live there for three years after they married. When Frances' father became too old to maintain the ranch, Melvin expressed interest in taking over. He leased it for awhile before buying it.

"The best part of ranching is being your own boss," Melvin explained. "I guess I thought it would be a pretty good life to live. Of course, you don't make any money. If you're in it for the money, forget it. You're not going to get it. If you want to be your own boss and are not afraid of hard work, it's a good life."

It takes a special breed to make a life on a ranch above 9,000 feet, especially during the mid-1900s when there wasn't electricity or running water in the remote parts of the County. The conditions were raw. There were drifts of snow up to 18-feet deep that could keep the Longs homebound for a week or more. Frances, who was all too familiar with passing long days cooped up during a winter storm, joked, "If I ever get to a point where I can't read, they may as well shoot me." In addition to reading, she would spend hours quilting or trying out new recipes.

"Francis and I have definitely spent some miserable times out there in that field with the wind blowin' and it snowin'," Melvin recalled. He said traveling to town in the winter was often treacherous. Frances remembers stories of her parents trying

Melvin Long working on an old wagon jack.

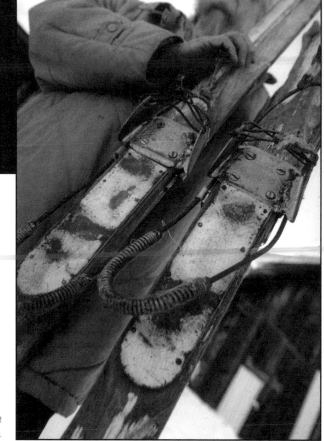

Frances Long and old 10th Mountain Division skis that belonged to her brother.

to prepare by stocking up on provisions such as 25 pounds of apricots, 600 pounds of flour and 500 pounds of sugar. Melvin recalls hearing that it cost $.50 for a shirt and $.75 for a pair of overalls. Many ranchers ordered most of their repair equipment from the Montgomery Ward catalog, including nuts, bolts and sickles. Occasionally they would go to Dillon for additional supplies. There was a general store ran by Pete Lege and another by Ed Riley. Sundreggers also had a general store that was in operation until the Dillon Dam was built.

Frances played an active role on the ranch at an early age and she's been riding a horse as long as she can remember. In the spring and fall the ranch children would ride horses to school. In the winter, they would drive a horse and "cutter" (sled) all the way to the Slate Creek school they attended. She learned to ride from her father, Alva Marshall, to whom horses were part of everyday life. Alva, along with another cowboy, would round up cattle belonging to a rancher named Andrew Lindstrom that ranged around the mining claims above Breckenridge. They would rope one steer at a time, tying them to trees until eventually they had the whole herd of cattle tied. Then they would come back collecting six to eight cows at a time, stringing them between two horses and taking them down the hill into town. It was typical for a heifer to stay in the low country grazing while a steer would head to the top of the hill to see how high he could get.

Melvin recalled Frances' father telling him there was no way a person could run a ranch without work horses. Melvin confessed that he hasn't put a harness on a horse since her dad died in 1968. While horses have long been instrumental to the working life of a ranch, modern machinery has made it more efficient.

> *"I can't say there's been anything outstanding,*
> *but it's been a happy existence.*
> *It's had its downs, yes,*
> *but it's had a lot of ups too."*

When the Long's daughter asked to go trail riding one visit, Melvin couldn't see the entertainment in it. " 'Pleasure ride?' I asked, 'What the devil is that?' When I get on a horse, I'm going to work. I'm not taking any pleasure ride," Melvin said.

Although it was hard work, branding was one of the most social events of the year. Once a year, in the spring, the same crew would work their way around neighboring ranches to help brand each other's cattle. It was a chance for the women to catch up and visit. At the end of a hard day's work, the women would have prepared a big feast with a roast, rolls, pies and drinks.

Frances Long's father driving cattle down
Ridge Street in Breckenridge in 1925.

The Slate Creek School circa 1928.
Frances Long is the second student from the right, standing.

While ranch life certainly was a 24-hour commitment of hard work to keep everything running smoothly, the Longs reminisce about the fun as well. Frances fondly describes moonlit nights in the winter when a group of friends would go tobogganing. She said they'd nearly freeze to death, "but it was good fun anyway."

Dancing provided another outlet for gathering and socializing. Melvin remembers the first time he met Karl Knorr, who would become his neighbor and one of the County's most senior residents. The VFW was hosting a dance with a local orchestra, but they were missing a drummer. Melvin had heard that his new neighbor played the drums, so he drove to the Knorr's house to recruit him. Karl was a hit.

In those days, people had to bring their own beverages to dances and rodeos. Between songs, they would go outside to their cars and wet their whistles. "That was one of the most fun aspects of the dance – when the whole gang would go out to the car to get a drink, mostly because we could sit around telling stories and laughing," said Melvin. Frances' dad once knew a man named Kennedy who made whisky with the label that read, "The only moonshine recommended by Dr. Smith." He would feed the whisky mash to his pigs to destroy any evidence in case the police stopped by. The pigs were always drunk and one sick calf actually died from a shot of the booze!

Taking a rare moment to ponder what life was like on the ranch, Frances said, "I can't say there's been anything outstanding, but it's been a happy existence. It's had its downs, yes, but it's had a lot of ups too."

Melvin simply said that if they didn't like it, they wouldn't be here. "We've had several offers to sell, but we're still here."

Trygve Berge

"I did somersaults every weekend up here for the tourists."

— *Trygve Berge on getting people excited about skiing*

It takes a true visionary to see something spectacular in the previously nonexistent and shape it to meet that dream. Trygve Berge possesses that rare talent. A stone mason by trade and an artist by hobby, Trygve financed his first trip to the United States by selling some of his original oil paintings in Norway. He later was involved in the development of one of the nation's most popular ski resorts – Breckenridge.

"We didn't know how big it was going to get," said Trygve.

Trygve grew up in Voss, Norway, in the same hometown that Breckenridge local Olav Pedersen grew up. In fact, it was Trygve who would later bring Olav to Breckenridge in 1964 to work with the newly forming ski school program. He also first met Freda Langell, a Keystone ski instructor, at the 1951 Norwegian Ski Championships in Molde, Norway. At one point he worked as a mountain guide with ropes in the Norwegian glaciers doing ice climbing in the summer months. "I have always believed in safety first, because I want to do this as long as I can." Over the years, however, more than 30 of Trygve's friends have died in avalanches. Like Olav and Freda, who have skiing in their blood, Trygve has long felt the influence of his Scandinavian heritage and began racing at a young age. "I'm not good at standing still," he said.

During his racing career, Trygve excelled at downhill competition. He remembers racing downhill in the 1956 Olympics in Cortina, Italy, because the course was so difficult that no one else wanted to tackle the challenge. Skiing with bear trap bindings before safety bindings were developed, there was a legitimate fear of injury. In 1949, in fact, Trygve did actually break his femur twice in one year. The first break occurred while he practiced slalom skiing and the second happened when he tried riding a bicycle before the leg had completely healed. The severity of his leg injury greatly hindered his progress as a skier.

Not one to give up easily, Trygve persevered. Through dedication to a sport he loved, he finally made the Norwegian Ski Team in 1954 and was back to skiing aggressively by 1955. He competed at Squaw Valley in the North American Championships, where he placed fourth. Trygve won four or five other races on the West Coast. The last international ski race that he won was a sanctioned World Cup race in the summer of 1958 in Norway. For a season or two, Trygve continued to race professionally when he had the time.

After the Olympics in 1956, he came to the United States with fellow Norwegian skier Stein Eriksen and headed to the popular California ski area Heavenly Valley, where he won a number of races. He briefly returned to Norway early in 1958 to ski with the Norwegian Ski Team again before moving to Aspen Highlands with Stein. It was in Aspen that the course of history was forever altered. Trygve met a man named Bill Rounds who had come to Aspen on a skiing holiday and who mentioned that his father who had purchased some land around the town of Breckenridge.

Bill Rounds, Celdin Catlin (the second manager of Breckenridge Lands Co.), Trygve Berge and Governor John Love in 1965 on the occasion of meeting to discuss the proposed Winter Olympic Games for Colorado.

Trygve and friend in 1939 at mock wedding which was part of the Honsok Celebration during the Midsummer's Night.

Trygve and family on their farm in Voss, Norway in 1935.

As fate would have it, Trygve accepted a job with the Rounds family to build a lumberyard in Breckenridge as well as a house for the manager. He remembers asking Bill, after the lumber business became operational, what they were going to do in the winter. Bill replied, "I don't know. Do you think we could ski?" With this seed planted and the thought of building some small cabins to accommodate skiing visitors, the Rounds family continued to acquire land whenever the opportunity arose.

A group of five that included Trygve and Bill, drove up an old Jeep trail to the location of the present-day Colorado SuperChair. They walked up the mountain and finally made their way to the top of Peak 8. Sitting on some old logs near the area where they had parked the Jeep, Bill pulled out some Cutty Sark, mixed it with some spring water and decided then and there to build a ski area. The next winter, Trygve went to Michigan to run the Boyne Mountain Ski School as a favor to Stein Eriksen. One day, Bill and Claude Martin, the Summit County Development Corporation Manager, stopped by on their drive back from Washington, D.C. to tell Trygve their journey had been a success – they had secured a permit to build a ski area. Breckenridge Ski Area would have to pay 3% of its revenues to the U.S. Forest Service (USFS) even though Arapahoe Basin was only paying 1.5%. Trygve remembers, "At that time, the Forest Service didn't even know what skiing was."

"I have always liked making skiing a social thing. And to be honest, I like to show off."

Everything seemed to move full-speed ahead once they secured the permit. In the spring of 1961, they began cutting trails and by December 17 of that year, they opened for business. Sigurd Rockne, the Colorado Ski School director for two seasons, and Trygve laid out all the runs and named most of them. Rounder is named after Bill Rounds and Cally's Alley is named for his wife. Springmeier was named after one of the old-time residents of Breckenridge, Al Springmeier, who owned a number of buildings in town. Trygve recalled, "Al would walk all the way to the Breckenridge Inn just to find a penny. He was a real character." Trygve also named the Bergenhof, which means "by the cliff" in Norwegian. It was designed at the request of Claude Martin, the first manager of Breckenridge, to be an alpine-styled lodge at the base of Peak 8. During the inaugural year, 1,800 people came to ski.

Ski Country USA, an organization that started not long after Breckenridge opened and began a tour of ski shows in the early and mid-1960s to promote skiing as a sport and pastime. Up until that time, skiing hadn't yet become popular, to which Trygve added, "It didn't come easy." He would play his clarinet at the Colorado Ski Follies with Max Dercum and do somersaults on crushed ice wearing 215 cm skis, putting his high school gymnastics training to use as a way to entertain the tourists and attract new skiers. "I did somersaults every weekend up here for the tourists," Trygve said. He attributes the growing interest in skiing to ski magazines and the increasing number of ski movies during the late '60s and '70s. In

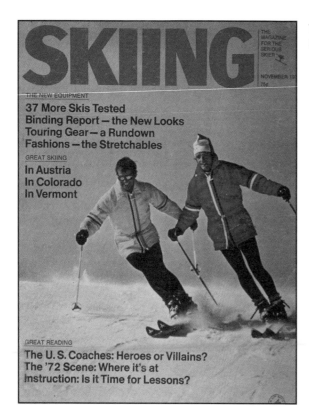

Trygve Berge skiing with Jean Claude Killy, *SKIING Magazine*, 1971.

Trygve Berge in front of his "meeting place" at Stein Eriksen's ski school at Aspen Highlands in 1959.

Trygve Berge jumping at Breckenridge in 1962.

the '70s, he skied for filmmaker Warren Miller on several occasions in Aspen, Boyne Mountain, Mammoth Mountain and Breckenridge. At one point, the Town of Breckenridge recruited Jean Claude Killy to be its spokesperson in about 1970. He was a also a guest trainer and instructor with Trygve a few times. When the word did finally spread, Breckenridge became known as the place to go when people wanted a low-key type hideout rather than to be "seen."

In 1961, Trygve opened the Norway Haus ski shop in the building the Steak and Rib now occupies. The shop later moved to the Salt Creek Saloon location and then to its present-day Main Street location. He owned 13 pairs of rental skis to begin with and the shop gradually grew. The shop began doing quite well in 1968 before more competition started moving in.

In the spring of 1976, he was pinned against the passenger side door of his car when a train hit his car during a Denver excursion and was almost killed. Once he recovered from his injuries, he opened another small ski shop in Breckenridge called Trygve's.

Today, Trygve claims to be more of a fair-weather skier now than he was during his years of adrenaline-pumping racing. He still enjoys the moguls of Breckenridge's double-diamond run Mach I but now he prefers it accompanied by a nice lunch and some togetherness with friends. "I have always liked making skiing a social thing," he said with a grin. "And to be honest, I like to show off."

After living in Summit County for the past 40 years, Trygve sees Colorado as a place to hang his hat. "I've been here so long, this feels more like home than any other place."

Billboard outside of Denver in 1963.

George and Susy Culbreath

"There were nine of us in my (high school) graduation class.
I've always said that I was the only one who stayed in the County
because there was only one job left."

—*George Culbreath on life in Summit County*

Pictures have the tremendous intensity of silence — a silence that speaks volumes about a person in the setting that has helped shape his character. To paint a picture of George Culbreath, one might depict calm in a man with unwavering core values and strong fundamental beliefs. It is a picture that also reflects the quiet resolve of Summit County.

The youngest of Cully and Elizabeth Culbreath's three children, George played well into the role of the much-adored baby of the family. Always a bit more mischievous than his siblings, he recalls once driving down Main Street Breckenridge in high school shooting out all six of the town's street lights. Another time, George hiked to the top of Mount Quandary and dragged an old miner's forge down the Blue Lakes side of the 14,000-foot mountain with the help of a burro.

Like his father, George has always possessed a certain charisma mixed with a practical ability to survive even when times were financially tough. While he was really too young to have felt the effects of the Green Mountain reservoir project, he does have vivid memories of his dad's dairy barn. As a child, the house he grew up in would get so cold that the linoleum flooring actually curled up each morning. He spent many hours in the barn with all its milking equipment, as it was the warmest place on the ranch. Yet, he remembers the amount of hard work that went into the 35-cow dairy and wasn't as taken with life as a rancher as his brother Grady. As a result, it would be Grady who took over the responsibilities of his father's ranch when the boys returned from the service in the late 1950s, while George pursued other means of making a living.

Over the years, George worked in many diverse capacities. He and Grady worked in the tunnels of the Wellington mine, shoveling ore onto muck sheets and filling many cars by hand. Breckenridge's economy became very depressed following the decline of the mining industry and had nearly returned to its ghost town state. George remembers hearing the painful sounds of the lode miners wheezing, infected with the ailment of miner's consumption in their lungs. For parts of two years, George also worked in the Roberts Tunnel, built to transport water from the bottom of Lake Dillon to Denver's South Platte River. Completed in 1960, the tunnel is 23 miles long. He remembers it being a great job, because the temperature under the Continental Divide was always a comfortable 56 degrees.

For several years, George was actively involved in bareback and saddle bronc riding and traveled around the state, competing on the rodeo circuit. Once riders acquired enough points from winning a few competitions, they were qualified to join the Professional Rodeo Cowboy Association (PRCA), as George did. It was hard to survive as a professional rodeo cowboy when contestants were required to pay $50 entry fees. Riders, like George, had to keep winning in order to pay for it. "I was never able to place at the big ones, but I did alright. I won a lot of the competitions, including the intercollegiate all-around." George explained, adding that he earned enough money riding to buy a new car.

Susy Culbreath
at 5 years old.

Susy at age 10
with Silver.

L-R: Gert (Young),
Grady and George
Culbreath at the
Otter Creek Ranch
in 1941.

George Culbreath
skiing at age 6.

"He was good – very good – but I still always held my breath when he rode," admitted Susy, who would watch the competitions from the stands toward the end of his career on the rodeo circuit.

Originally from Michigan, Susy and her friend Shirley Snyder, who now lives in Frisco, packed up with California dreams and headed West. Taken by the beauty of Colorado, they altered their plans in order to stay in the Rocky Mountains and considered teaching positions in a small mining town, Uravan, located 60 miles from Montrose. Susy explained, "We stayed with an Indian family. They treated us royally, because they wanted young teachers in the school system, but it was just too far away from everything."

They moved to teach at Climax from 1957 to 1958 and discovered a wonderful, friendly group of people that welcomed them in. At 19 and 21 respectively, Susy accepted a first grade teaching job and Shirley took one teaching kindergarten. "We had the best time up there," recalled Susy. "We would go skiing on weekends and night skiing some. Afterward, we would gather at the warming hut where Bob Zdechlik would entertain us." While she was still learning how to ski, Susy earned the nickname "rubberlegs" from Marie Zdechlik, who was a very accomplished skier. Shirley ended up marrying the superintendent's son and Susy returned to Michigan briefly to finish her degree at Western Michigan University in Kalamazoo. She later taught two more years in Dillon where the dam was being built.

"I've never been opposed to growth.
I guess it paid off to hang around."

The 1950s, post-war "happy days" with good music and fun times, gave leisure activities, such as skiing, increased popularity. "My folks thought skiing was a fad and would pass," recalled George, who raced in high school and later in college for Colorado State University. A lover of speed with natural athletic ability, George raced with many junior national champions from the strong European countries in the slalom, giant slalom and downhill events. He also competed on the old ski jump at Dillon in various college meets.

Skiing began catching on in the '50s in Summit County, but there weren't the crowds that exist on the slopes of the resorts today. "The skiing was excellent. You could ski from the top of the mountain to the bottom without worrying about hitting anyone," recalled George. It was on one of those days skiing at Climax that he first met his sister Gert's roommate, Susanne Randall. During this time, he and Susy became friends and enjoyed many of the same outdoor activities, such as horseback riding, hiking and fishing. They married in 1961, raised three children and recently celebrated their 38th wedding anniversary. George smiles and says their feelings obviously changed from being just friends.

Saddle that George won for All Around Cowboy at the CSU Skyline Stampede in 1961.

George Culbreath at the Greeley Stampede in 1958.

When he completed his tour of duty, George returned to make a life in Summit County. "There were nine of us in my (high school) graduation class. I've always said that I was the only one who stayed in the county because there was only one job left," said George. George and Susy lived in the old lodge at Cataract Lake the first winter after they were married. In March 1962, they moved to their present location at Rocky Nob Ranch. Deciding that they really didn't own enough acres to make a living as ranchers, George decided to try the construction business.

With the purchase of their first tractor in 1963, George and Susy started Culbreath Excavating, which they owned and operated for 14 years. The company grew to 20 employees and was involved in a lot of the early construction at Keystone and Copper Mountain. "We got married, had our first daughter, bought a ranch and started a new business all in a relatively short period of time," remarked Susy. "It was a lot to have happening at once."

The Culbreath family was actively involved in the Kremmling area. Their children attended school there and they were involved in sports and 4-H. The family also attended the Kremmling Community Church. Their leisure time was often spent hiking and backpacking in the Gore Range. George and Susy remember when they and their children set out on a three-day trek from their house over the Gore Range to Vail. It was a great trip, but by the end they were ready to hit the hot tub at Vail and eat a good meal.

Both George and Susy acknowledge that there was plenty of blood, sweat and tears that went into living in Summit County over the years, but there was also contentment. Glancing out their picture window at the lush Blue River valley, they thank God for the privilege of living there. "There are so many memories for us in Summit County. This is where we met and where we raised our children," George said.

❄

Gertrude Philippe

"It wasn't a question of being hermits. We just wanted to be outdoors."

—*Getrude Philippe on why she and husband Frank chose to build a cabin in Frisco*

What began as a fun, weekend getaway nearly 54 years ago — just a small cabin in the woods — has since transformed into so much more. It has become a home full of memories and experiences and a legacy to pass on to a new generation.

During World War II, Gertrude Philippe was hired as a civilian in the small arms ammunition division of Remington Arms while her husband, Frank, was stationed in Sacramento as a member of the Signal Corps. When he was transferred to Camp Livingston in Louisiana, Gertrude joined him, explaining that she "was bored and didn't want to sit around. It just isn't my style. So even though I had no experience working with guns, the recruiter saw 'small arms' on my record and took me in." She added that it was to her benefit that she was good at memorizing parts. Again, when they were transferred to Camp Shanks, New York, they needed money and Gertrude wanted something to do. She used her experience with small arms and learned how to balance trigger weights so triggers wouldn't creep. She remembers a soldier pointing to her saying, "That girl can fix guns that will make me a marksman."

In 1946, with peacetime settling across the country, Gertrude and Frank became an anomaly among their friends in Denver. Very few people immediately following World War II were second-home owners. "It was not so fashionable then," admitted Gertrude, but explained that she and her husband led such active social lives in Denver, that they were searching for a place where they could escape – a place to "get away from it all" and do all the things they loved to do, such as horseback riding.

The Philippes originally came to Summit County to visit Elmer Swanson and his family for a weekend. Elmer owned the store and property that would later become the Foote's Rest, after he sold it to Helen and Bob Foote. Through Elmer's encouragement, Gertrude and Frank went in with Gertrude's sister Sarah and John Finesilver to purchase six lots in Frisco for a grand total of $150 ($25 each) and then celebrated ownership by going fishing. While fishing may seem like a humorous way, perhaps, to acknowledge the purchase of mountain property, it was a favorite pastime of the Philippes. They preferred Wheeler Ponds and Rainbow Lake to the Blue River and always caught their limit of brook and rainbow trout.

"We would pan fry fish in our outdoor fireplace," explained Gertrude. "It was one of the first things we built because we loved to cook over an open flame and we didn't have a stove until we finished the cabin."

When they were ready to begin building, Elmer Swanson had made arrangements for the U.S. Forest Service to mark logs, including a 30-foot ridge pole, to be used in the construction of their cabin. Possessing many useful skills in the ways of the mountains, Elmer advised that they build their house with their front porch facing south to prevent too much snow from accumulating. Gertrude and Sarah hand-peeled all of the logs. They also gathered and washed all the rocks for the fireplace, but hired someone to build it. Their basement was so cool that Gertrude would store milk or other perishables down there

Gertrude Philippe, third from left, front row, in top photo
working on the cabin in 1946.

and they would keep. It wasn't until 1981 that they installed a furnace exclusively as a heat source. Even during the winter they relied on the fireplace. Her son Rob, who now uses the cabin as his primary residence, has since added a master bedroom and a kitchen among other modern conveniences, onto the original structure. Later he added four more bedrooms, three baths and a library.

"There really wasn't any help up here and we were amateurs," said Gertrude. They dug their own well, but it was shallow — only eight or 10 feet — so they relied on an outhouse, which still stands on their property today. Each year they would get their water tested for contaminants to make sure it was safe. Through a friend's generous donation of a coal-burning stove with a water jack, the two families always had hot water.

"I thought it was rugged here with all the deer and the mountain lions. I liked to hike, fish and I have always loved the mountains," said Gertrude. "We were outdoor people. We came here to get away from the world." She remembers crying when they put the road in, which was before skiing really entered the County. She had always felt like their cabin was a glorified version of camping when they came up from Denver. "I knew we were no longer camping when the street light was put in," Gertrude added.

---

*"We were outdoor people.
We came here to get away from the world."*

While they maintained a primary residence in Denver and visited Summit County mostly on weekends, the Philippes have strong ties to the Rocky Mountain heritage. Frank's great-grandfather Solomon Philippe, a saloon owner, came to Leadville in the 1800s. In keeping with this spirit of western exploration, Gertrude and Frank loved to go off-road in their '46 Jeep Willy, driving as high as the roads would take them. They would wander around Peak 10 and the Briar Rose mine before anything was there, often collecting bottles and other items that had been discarded by the miners that had ventured onto the land before them. Today, they have an entire wall covered with pioneer memorabilia. One prized piece they uncovered was an old cowbell that Gertrude would ring standing on her porch in order to get her two boys inside for dinner.

In the winter months, Gertrude and her family enjoyed snow-shoeing, both for recreation as well as necessity. "We purchased a few pairs of snowshoes at the Army surplus store because the snow was so deep," said Gertrude. When they were bringing loads of groceries or other items into the house, they often used a sled. Beginning with ski areas at Arapahoe Basin, followed by Breckenridge and then Keystone, it was an exciting time to watch Summit County being transformed into a recreational paradise. "We were very enthusiastic about skiing," Gertrude recalled.

The cabin built by the Philippes in 1946
before the building of Frisco Street.

Gertrude (Miller)
Philippe in 1935.

They came up almost every weekend and every spring break by driving over Loveland Pass, which was still a dirt road. Gertrude described some harrowing journeys when someone had to walk out in front of the car to help them from running off the road during near white-out conditions. Gertrude would often come up during the week as well, with the children and then Frank would join them on weekends when he had completed work at the Columbia Press, Inc., which he owned. A self-described "city gal," Gertrude still reminisces about her time in Summit County and says, "It is just a great place to be. We're here by choice. If we didn't like it, we would have never come at all and put forth all this time and effort."

Her son Rob, born in 1949, became a commercial real estate developer and had the vision to purchase property on Main Street in Frisco in anticipation of the growth potential of ski country. He purchased all the land on Main Street from the ReMax real estate building, which once was Sue Chamberlain's former house, all the way to the corner where the Frisco Hotel is located. Among his first projects was the construction of the restaurant/bar Charity's that existed for 18 years until last August when the bar underwent new ownership and became Tuscato's. Rob later won awards for historic restoration for his work on an 1875 locomotive, the oldest in the state, that is now stored in his antique barn, as well as for work on an 1881 Pullman car that once ran through Frisco. Today he and his mother have 60 permanent tenants leasing property from them. Gertrude handles all the bookkeeping, a skill she acquired from a talented auditor who worked with the family company.

"If we had bought land instead of printing presses, we'd have been better off," said Gertrude reflecting back on career choices with the present knowledge of Summit County's real estate boom and the increase in land values.

When Frank retired, he and Gertrude volunteered with the International Executive Service Corps (IESC), an organization of retired executives who volunteer to give expertise to other executives in developing countries. From 1974 to 1984, they traveled to Mexico, Venezuela, Columbia, Indonesia and Trinidad. Gertrude also volunteered with the American Women's organizations of these countries doing various projects.

After Frank died, Gertrude remarried in 1987 to a concert violinist and music instructor, Bert Naster. At one point in his career, he played with the Denver Symphony during his 53 years of orchestra performance. "Part of our prenuptial agreement was that Gertrude learn how to ski," Bert joked.

With a smile, thinking of all the fun she and her family had in their Summit County refuge, Gertrude said, "When I die, no one will be able to say I led a dull life."

❅

Jim and Maureen Nicholls

"When you wanted dry cleaning done you would put a sign in your window for the dry cleaner to stop by. They would just drive up and down the street looking for signs."

—Maureen Nicholls on life in Breckenridge in the 1960s

The 1960s represented a decade of new discoveries – an "out with the old, in with the new" cleansing of sorts for the nation. While both Jim and Maureen (Sloan) Nicholls arrived independently to Summit County during this period of rapid change, they have always shared a fundamental love of the high country and a loyalty to Breckenridge. Maureen believed the past was well worth preserving and today champions bygone eras through ownership of Quandary Antiques, a shop that began 19 years ago in Breckenridge. Over the years, Maureen has repeatedly been recognized for her countless hours of volunteer work with the Summit Historical Society. Jim has spent much of his time working in organizations promoting Breckenridge's economy. Predicting the County's future growth, Jim once said, "This place is going to be something someday." He now spends his time at his art gallery/western artifact shop, Paint Horse Gallery. When Quandary Antiques moved to it's new location on Ridge Street, the gallery replaced it in their yellow Victorian on Main Street.

Although Jim Nicholls grew up in Gary, Indiana, his great-grandfather emigrated to Colorado in 1878 and mined at the boom towns in Ten Mile Canyon, Leadville and Cripple Creek Mining District. Jim joined his parents on family vacations in Fruita during the summer, went to college in Fort Collins and came to Summit County in 1961 searching for a couple of lots for his parents' retirement setting. At the time, there were only about 250 people living in Breckenridge, but with the Dillon Dam under construction, land values were expected to rise as the area gained in popularity. When he walked into Summit County Development Company's (SCDC) office on Main Street Breckenridge to inquire about lots, he noticed an empty drafting desk. He remembers asking the manager, Claude Martin, "Who sits there?" to which Claude replied "No one." Less than 15 days later, with two feet of snow welcoming him on Labor Day, Jim took a job with SCDC and moved to Breckenridge.

With the dredges long gone and drab rock piles everywhere leaving a memorial to the once flourishing mining industry, Breckenridge languished as not much more than a shell of a town before skiing revitalized the economy. "People had let vacant land go for delinquent tax sales, particularly mining claims, thinking the area would never amount to anything," explained Jim.

Seeing future potential, Jim's first Breckenridge employer, Rounds and Porter Lumber, a company from Wichita, Kansas, entered the picture and began buying up parcels of land for only $55 per acre until they had accumulated 5,500 acres in and around Breckenridge. SCDC even set up an office in the old courthouse to facilitate this process. Bill Rounds, having spent time skiing in Aspen, liked the idea of a quaint but timeworn mining town close to Denver in which to invest his family's money.

With Arapahoe Basin, Loveland, Cooper Hill and Climax paving the way, skiing was catching on in Colorado and it wasn't long before the idea to develop a ski area at Breckenridge emerged. Vail was also starting its beginning planning stages and

Maureen Nicholls on the right in her NSPS uniform in front of the Bergenhof building at Breckenridge in 1965.

Jim and Maureen Nicholls skiing Breckenridge in 1966.

the two areas raced to see which mountain opened first. Breckenridge won and planned its grand opening on December 16, 1961. A member of Colorado State's ski club in college, Jim showed much enthusiasm for the ski area's development and was asked to perform a number of duties in preparation for its opening. He drew up plans for the first on-mountain warming hut, which moved to several locations before succumbing to a restaurant fire on Main Street, Breckenridge in 1997. Bill Rounds asked Jim to paint a six-foot sign that resembled an official highway marker with just the word "Breckenridge" and a giant arrow. Late one night they surreptitiously posted the sign at the junction of Highways 6 and 40 (now I-70), west of Idaho Springs, as a way to attract travelers to the budding resort. That sign remained in place for more than 12 years. As assistant to the manager of SCDC, Jim's position as a "gofer" meant also finding out where Rounds and Porter's 5,500 acres lay, and the best use for the land.

"Perhaps one of the most memorable times in my life was the night before the lifts opened," recalled Jim. He gathered with 15 people around a fireplace at a popular bar and restaurant called The Mine on Main Street. With the snow falling heavily outside, and everyone singing and listening to Eric Laurence's piano playing, the festivities continued until 4 in the morning. That first year of operation, 18,000 lift tickets were sold at $3.50 each!

After leaving SCDC, known as Breckenridge Lands, Inc. today, Jim worked for Fitzhugh Scott, the early architect of Vail, and commuted over Vail Pass on Highway 6. It wasn't long before staying in Breckenridge appealed more to him and Jim opened his architecture/design office, the only such firm in Summit County, working at first out of his home. In 1963, Jim purchased a log cabin at 302 South Ridge Street where the Nicholls still reside. Three additions have been added since the Breckenridge Volunteer Fire Department built the cabin in 1955, originally for a charity raffle. His first remodel project involved building the fireplace, laboriously hauling quartz moss rock from high on Peak 10 to create its rugged appeal. The mantle beam was dragged from the Ware-Carpenter smelter located across the Blue River where Sawmill Creek Condos now reside on Park Avenue and Ski Hill Road. Seeking steadier winter income, Jim joined the Breckenridge Ski School and taught for three years.

Originally from Marquette, Michigan, Maureen Sloan worked as a childrens counselor at a dude ranch in the Sangre De Cristos Mountains of Colorado between her freshman and sophomore year of college. Falling in love with the state, she vowed that after graduation she would teach in Detroit, buy her first car and move to Colorado. In 1963, Maureen moved to Colorado Springs to teach history and English for three years. During that time she passed the National Ski Patrol test and began volunteering at Breckenridge Ski Area on weekends. Growing up in the North, she had been skiing since she was only 4 years old.

Even though patrollers and ski school instructors didn't mingle much socially, Jim and Maureen's paths eventually crossed. With five other teachers, Maureen rented the house that is now Bubba's Bones restaurant on Ridge Street for the winter of 1965-66. That January, Jim and Maureen went on their first date and married five months later, in June.

Jim Nicholls at the Ullr Dag
celebration in 1966.

Jim Nicholls' original ski school patch.
Maureen Nicholls' Breckenridge patch
with the original sunburst design, both from
the early days of Breckenridge. Maureen's
NSPS patch in the background.

Maureen continued to patrol until 1969, even when she was pregnant with the first of their three daughters. "Everyone on the mountain was in a lottery as to which run my baby would be born," Maureen recalled. "They would make up names for the baby like Mach 1 Nicholls or Tiger Nicholls." In the seventh month of her pregnancy, the pro patrol finally took her boots away and told her she couldn't ski anymore until after the baby was born.

In the late 1960s, as president of Breckenridge's Chamber of Commerce, Jim led the town clean-up, an event where members of the community pitched in to beautify the town. Governor John Love honored Breckenridge with an award for outstanding civic improvement and invited Jim to the state capitol to receive it. Jim said, "We tore down all kinds of old sheds and hauled away about 35 old wrecked cars. It was the most successful clean up we ever had in this town." Maureen counters with a laugh, "What a change. Now it's preserve, preserve, preserve."

Jim and Maureen purchased the old historic C.A. Finding Hardware building on Main Street and moved Jim's design business there. Soon real estate, property management and building "spec" houses were integrated with his house designing. Relocating several times, finally into an 1899 house at 224 South Main Street, led to another career change in 1987. Jim, encouraged by his father, a lifelong artist, opened the Paint Horse Gallery.

During 12 years in the 1970s and 1980s, Jim served on the Breckenridge Planning Commission. Later he joined forces with several other businessmen to form the Breckenridge Business Association as a lobby group that opposed mandatory parking quotas for each new business. In order to provide the required parking, it would have been necessary to tear down old buildings, which the town was encouraging owners to preserve. A plan was devised for a parking district that finally became ordinance in 1998. Rounding out his community involvement in those early years, Jim volunteered 18 years as a firefighter and also served on the Town of Dillon's architectural review board, about which he said, "There really wasn't a board. I was it. They would show designs to me and I'd say yes or no. It was pretty primitive."

After they were married, Maureen continued her teaching career at Summit High and then substituted for several years after their daughters Kristie, Carrie and Jill were born in Fairplay, the nearest hospital. With no day-care in Summit County except for a few older women providing it in their homes, Maureen gave up teaching except for local history classes at Colorado Mountain College (CMC). Nevertheless, it wasn't unusual for residents of Summit County to dabble in a little bit of everything to sustain the lifestyle they loved so much. Maureen, further diversifying her resumé, even operated a bed and breakfast for five years at their home for additional income.

Living so close to Main Street when everything south of Washington Avenue was residential, Jim and Maureen became acquainted with many old-timers who still longed "to get underground" and mine and who didn't appreciate the new "slope dope" economy, as they called it, that skiing attracted. They frequently befriended these elderly residents and took a keen interest in their stories of days gone by. Maureen and Jim helped them clean out old barns, paint their walls, repair leaking

Jim Nicholls in the
Paint Horse Gallery
in Breckenridge.

Maureen Nicholls at her
shop, Quandary Antiques,
in Breckenridge.

roofs and help with their garage sales. Soon, the Nicholls became the recipients of discarded, but desirable, memorabilia and antiques – regarded as junk then.

Through this new hobby, Maureen discovered her next career – Quandary Antiques – a shop that would allow her to combine the love of history with old artifacts. At a workshop offered by the State Historical Society that she attended, one of the speakers advised, "Get out and photograph your mountain towns, because they're the ones changing so fast." Although she regrets not taking any pictures of the bulldozing of the old dredge rock piles along the Blue River in town, an event she knew to be significant, she did photograph Breckenridge beginning in the early 1970s thanks to her enrollment in CMC photography classes. Jim also took slides of the developing of the Breckenridge Ski Area in its earliest days. These photographs, along with Maureen's large collection of 1880s to 1930s Breckenridge photos, are treasured possessions, and necessitate many sessions in Maureen's darkroom.

Jim and Maureen have indeed seen many changes in the area, including the opening and dedication of Swan Mountain Road which made travel to Denver over Loveland Pass a shorter journey. They remember when the Breckenridge bowling alley was one of the most popular recreational spots in the County. Beyond Cully Culbreath delivering milk door-to-door, shopping was a much bigger challenge for locals then unless they were looking for ski gear. "If you wanted to buy anything practical, you had to go to the Frisco Drug Store or to Leadville, a much larger town in the '60s and '70s than today," recalled Maureen. However, there was a dry cleaning service that did home pickups. "When you wanted dry cleaning done, you would put a sign in your window for the dry cleaner to stop by. They would just drive up and down the street looking for signs," Maureen said.

Festivals and celebrations have long been important to Breckenridge residents' sense of community. "Ullr Dag," a day to pay praise to the Norwegian god of winter, was one such event, but ceased for 10 years after the 1969 winter carnival got too wild. Breckenridge has capitalized on the Ullr slogan "The Kingdom of Breckenridge." Maureen explained that the "No Man's Land" celebration began when it was "discovered," however erroneously by the Breckenridge Women's Club, that cartographers omitted Breckenridge from maps after the Louisiana Purchase.

Today Maureen and Jim continue to live in town and enjoy walking everywhere. They glance around at a place that has evolved dramatically since they first arrived many years ago. While they embrace the changes of a new era and the prosperity that has accompanied it, they agree was fun to grow up with the town while their memories of the old and a little down-at-the-heel Breckenridge of the past remain special.

❄

Sena Valaer

"We were going to get married on the first of March, but we decided to wait
until the 10th of March because that was Johnny's birthday.
After the wedding, we came home and milked the cows."

—Sena Valaer on her wedding day with John Valaer

Perhaps there is no one better than Sena Valaer to exemplify the homily, "Bloom where you're planted." Born in Breckenridge in 1919, Sena has spent almost her entire life in Summit County and has flourished in every setting and every experience she has encountered.

Sena's tenacity may have come from her maternal grandfather, Lars Christensen, who came to the United States as a stowaway aboard a ship transporting cattle to the "New World." He worked his way across the country until he reached Denver, where he married. Moving to Summit County, the Christensens homesteaded a ranch in 1903 on a hill by the Slate Creek schoolhouse in the Lower Blue. They also had a mining claim in Breckenridge. Her paternal grandparents, the Ottersons, were Norwegian and also homesteaded a ranch, but it was along the Green River in Wyoming. Then in 1916, her parents met at Mrs. Black's Boarding House in Montezuma. Mrs. Black, a nurse, had two houses on Washington Street in Breckenridge where Sena's mother, and later Sena, were both born.

"I didn't know how to milk cows, drive a car or anything
when I first got married.
I was just a little high school gal."

As a young girl, Sena and her family, with three girls and one boy, moved several times between Laramie, Wyoming, Breckenridge and the Lower Blue. Sena remembers her father trapping coyotes on their ranch near the Green River and selling their pelts. She only went to school one year in Wyoming before they moved back to Colorado where her parents leased a ranch, Coal Place, near the old State Creek school. While there, her father served as a guide and would take people, by wagon, fishing to nearby lakes.

Sena attended Slate Creek school until the eighth grade before returning to her birthplace of Breckenridge for high school. In 1938, Sena graduated in the same class with her brother, Herman, who was just a year older. "He was my big buddy all through school," Sena remembers. Not long after graduation, he went to Pearl Harbor to serve in the Navy during World War II, but was lucky to be out at sea the morning the Japanese attacked.

Sena Valaer, age 9, and brother Herman on the way to school.

Sena Valaer and husband John shortly after they were married, circa 1939.

Sena Valaer (#9, fourth from left standing) and Breckenridge High School girl's basketball team, 1935-36.

Even at an early age, Sena learned the value of hard work. The Depression years were very difficult and everyone had to do their part. From 1936 to 1937, while she was still in high school, Sena helped in the kitchen of a private home on High Street where the owners, Mr. and Mrs. Harris, served boarders family-style meals. Sena smiles remembering that Mr. Harris was the only one allowed to mash the potatoes for dinner, because he did it best. Once a week, a man named Red Irving arrived from Kremmling to show a movie at The Mines Theater on Main Street in Breckenridge and then stay over night at the Harris' home. The movies then were all in black and white.

Sena also assisted Belle Marz, who had a wooden leg, and her husband, Joe, in The Brown Hotel kitchen. They used canned milk instead of fresh milk, so Sena cleverly began saving the coupons off the milk labels and eventually had enough to receive a free set of dishes in exchange. She still has that original set of eight floral-patterned china in her cupboard. After she graduated from high school in the summer of 1938, Sena went to work in another kitchen for The Hamilton Hotel in Dillon, later known as The Dillon Hotel. The owners, Mr. and Mrs. Briggs, also served roomers and boarders from the Green Mountain dam and reservoir, family-style. "I really learned a lot from all those places I worked," recalled Sena, who spoke not just of the skills inside the kitchen, but of other life lessons as well.

"There always seemed to be a wiener roast or something social for everyone."

Even during the Depression, people in Summit County found time for fun and laughter. Dances were at the center of the social scene, held throughout the County at various halls or schools. It was while attending a dance in Frisco with another date that Sena encountered the charms of John Valaer, who drove a dump truck for the construction crew working on Loveland Pass. When he politely offered her a ride home that evening, she accepted, as well as his proposal for marriage some time later. At 19 years old, Sena married John in Leadville. "We were going to get married on the first of March, but we decided to wait until the 10th of March because that was Johnny's birthday," said Sena. "After the wedding, we came home and milked the cows."

John's parents emigrated from Switzerland in 1905. His father moved to the United States to mine in Breckenridge and returned to Europe to get married. He brought his Swiss bride back to Summit County to see how she would like the mountain lifestyle. Unable to speak English, she would take notes to the grocery store to help her communicate with the clerks. In 1916, not long after they purchased the Roberts Ranch, Mrs. Valaer's husband died, forcing her to raise their children and maintain a full working ranch on her own. When Sena and John married, they helped with many of the ranch

Sena Valaer, far right, with friends Ray and Millie Hille, who owned The Dillon Inn.

chores. "I didn't know how to milk cows, drive a car or anything when I first got married," admitted Sena. "I was just a little high school gal." Always a quick learner, Sena soon became a valuable asset on the ranch. Mrs. Valaer taught her how to prepare a number of Swiss recipes, such as potato cakes, Swiss meatballs and knudley (liver). Sena took an interest in gardening as well and planted a variety of vegetables in the back of Mrs. Valaer's house, including cauliflower, cabbage, carrots and parsnips.

Amidst work on the ranch, attending rodeos became a popular pastime. Sena belonged to a saddle club and rode in a quadrille team, which is essentially like square dancing on horseback. Howard Giberson and Gail Byers were both actively involved in quadrille shows as well. Sena often rode Dick or Dan, two horses borrowed from a corral owned by Paul Dahl. She recalls getting bucked off in the middle of one performance, but as she had been instructed, she jumped right back on and continued with the show. "It was a lot of fun," said Sena. "I really enjoyed it and the gatherings afterwards. There always seemed to be a wiener roast or something social for everyone."

"We would host dinners to raise money or set up tables with cookies, cup cakes and coffee at rest stops on Vail Pass to do the good neighborly thing."

For seven years, Sena peddled milk in Dillon and took over the Breckenridge route when Mat Nicholson, who previously had that territory, wanted out of the business. Mrs. Valaer sold several different products, including whole milk, cream, butter and cottage cheese, to their customers throughout the County. John built a dam over Willow Creek to create the necessary pressure to force water into the house through special piping in order to facilitate a cooling process. Then the milk was bottled. The back seat of Sena's Chevy had been removed in order to stack boxes containing two dozen bottles per crate for delivery. In those days, a gallon of milk cost $.60, a half-gallon $.35, $.15 for a quart and $.50 for a pint of cream. "In all the years I delivered milk, I only had one customer who didn't pay his bill," Sena said.

John worked furiously cleaning the barn and feeding the cattle while Sena completed her route. When she returned, she helped him haul hay into the barn and grain the cows. "There was a lot of work involved with all of that," said Sena. In 1945, they sold the ranch to Cully Culbreath who took over the dairy operations.

Moving to Dillon in 1945, Sena joined the Rebekah Lodge and was accompanied by Martha Enyeart to her initiation in Leadville at a sister lodge. "We would host dinners to raise money or set up tables with cookies, cup cakes and coffee at rest stops on Vail Pass to do the good neighborly thing," she explained. Sena enjoyed learning where all the travelers were from. Once, she introduced children from South Africa to their very first marshmallow roast when they stopped at the rest area.

Sena Valaer and her
high school graduation
photo.

While John and Sena lived in Dillon in the 1950s, they bought The Mint pool hall and remodeled it, putting rooms upstairs and living there for awhile. They later rented the building out to a few different tenants. While John ran the pool hall, Sena began working at the Old Dillon Inn when the owner of the Dillon Garage asked her if she would run his liquor store. He was a Mason and it was frowned upon to possess a liquor license, so he eventually sold the store to Sena.

Then, Al Kucach, another local owner, offered Sena the opportunity to purchase a second liquor store, to combat a competitor. He told her to just "pay when she could." With so many construction crews working in the County to build the dam and the Roberts Tunnel, there arose a need for an accessible place to cash checks. The nearest bank was in Kremmling, so Sena began cashing checks for $.25 apiece. Every Friday night after payday, the construction workers would stand in a long line outside Sena's store. She also took cash from the post office as well as the school's hot lunch program to the Bank of Kremmling for deposit. "I had a good hiding place," said Sena. She was aware, however, of the potential dangers of being the sole person responsible for such large quantities of cash. One night, she remembers hearing gunshots that woke her up. She looked out her window to see a small group of men at the Dillon Inn with their hands in the air. The robber escaped, but authorities later discovered he had been an ex-con working in the tunnel.

In 1961, with the newly built Dillon Dam forcing local residents to move, the Valaers jacked up their home, put it on wheels and moved it to new Dillon. Residents were given salvage value if they weren't willing to move their house when the dam was built. "I wouldn't want to do it again," Sena said, remembering how difficult it was to relocate. Once in the new location, the house was remodeled inside and out and a front addition was built.

While they lived in their new Dillon location, John was still working for the County, plowing snow, which began as a nice gesture and turned into a full-time occupation. Sena and John spent 32 and a half wonderful years together, and had many colorful tales to tell before he died in 1971. Sena started her liquor store in the new town of Dillon in 1963, and sold it in 1967. She then went to work for the Little Brown Drug store in Dillon until 1983, and she always enjoyed talking to and interacting with customers.

Sena acknowledges that she has always been quite "ornery," but it might just be that spunk that has kept her young at heart all these years. She and her good friend Grace Warren earned a reputation for playing many a practical joke on acquaintances in town. "You have to make fun of yourself," said Sena thinking on her many experiences in Summit County over the years. "Life's too short to not have a little fun out of it."

❄

Afterward

In being offered the opportunity to write this book, I had the good fortune of being in the right place at the right time. As the newest member of Wilson · Lass' creative team and one of Summit County's greenest residents, I was an unlikely author of an historical collection of biographies. Nevertheless, my eagerness and willingness to take on the project must have made a convincing argument. I would like to personally extend my gratitude to the 26 featured individuals, our "contemporary pioneers," for inviting Bob and me into their homes and sharing a small taste of their experiences and memories of Summit County as it once was. Had they not lived the lives they did, and agreed to talk with us about them, the book would not exist. I have learned more than just about time and place events, but perhaps have gained some greater insight into the driving forces behind them – the things that are ultimately more important to people. Summit County should not, then, be boiled down to ranches, mines and ski resorts, but to the underlying passion, determination and love to make a life here. *Summit Pioneers* belongs to these individuals. It is their book, in that sense, more than it is mine, the photographer's or the creative agency's. As author Sebastian Junger once observed, "Writers don't often know much about the world they're trying to describe, but they don't necessarily need to. They just need to ask a lot of questions. And then they need to step back and let the stories speak for themselves."

Thank you for an experience I will never forget.

Alison Grabau